The 'Baby Killers'

...the little island set in the silver seas was at the end of its immunity...

H G Wells, *The War in the Air*

THE
'BABY KILLERS'

GERMAN AIR RAIDS ON BRITAIN
IN THE FIRST WORLD WAR

Thomas Fegan

Leo Cooper

For my mother and father

011803725

First published in Great Britain in 2002 by
Leo Cooper
an imprint of Pen & Sword Books Limited
47 Church Street, Barnsley, South Yorkshire, S70 2AS

ISBN 0-85052-893-3

A CIP catalogue record of this book
is available from the British Library

Printed by CPI UK

Contents

Acknowledgements

My sincere thanks go to the staff of various local and national museums, libraries and record offices for their help in providing me with information. Those at the Department of Documents and the Photograph Archive of the Imperial War Museum deserve special credit for their assistance over some time. Among the many individuals to whom I am indebted, personal mention must be made of Hazel Basford and Denise Rayner, and I am particularly obliged to Tom Hartman, my editor, for his scrutiny and patience, although any remaining mistakes are, of course, my own. I would also like to warmly acknowledge my wife Sophie for her suggestions and overall support.

Every effort has been made to obtain permission to use copyright material. I am deeply grateful to the Trustees of the Imperial War Museum for allowing access to their collections, and to the individual copyright holders who have kindly given me their consent to quote from the Papers of Lance Corporal H. H. Appleton, Lieutenant A. J. Arkell, Colonel E. B. Bartley, V. Bawtree, E. S. Bennett, P. Blundstone, M. Dayrell-Browning, Major T. Gran, H. Ingleby MP, Sir Clive Morrison-Bell, Private J. W. Mudd, J. H. Stapley and Ordinary Seaman F. W. Turpin.

THE FLIGHT THAT FAILED.

THE EMPEROR. "WHAT! NO BABES, SIRRAH?"
THE MURDERER. "ALAS! SIRE, NONE."
THE EMPEROR. "WELL, THEN, NO BABES, NO IRON CROSSES."

[*Exit murderer, discouraged.*

Cartoon from **Punch,** *January 1915.* **Punch** Publications

CHAPTER 1

The Threat From Above and Britain's Defences

But what would be the security of the good, if the bad could at pleasure invade them from the sky? Against an army sailing through the clouds neither walls, nor mountains, nor seas, could afford any security. A flight of northern savages might hover in the wind, and light at once with irresistible violence upon the capital of a fruitful region that was rolling under them.
Samuel Johnson, *Rasselas, The Prince of Abissinia*

The German air raids of the Great War were the first of their kind. Strategic aerial bombing had never been used before and its novelty was shocking. It was viewed as terrorism rather than a legitimate act of war. It caused panic and outrage far in excess of the death and material loss that was inflicted and its psychological impact was as great as that produced by the far more devastating Blitz of the Second World War. Britons were appalled that civilians were imperilled as much as soldiers. The 'baby killers', as the raiders were branded, brought dismay to a nation unaccustomed to fighting at home, and confirmed that the fortress isle was no longer safe from the hand of war.

Ever since the Frenchman Louis Blériot made the first aeroplane flight across the English Channel on 25 July 1909, H. G. Wells wrote in the *Daily Mail*, Britain was

Illustration by A. C. Michael for H. G. Wells' The War in the Air, depicting the massed fleet of German airships as it crosses the industrial Midlands.
British Library

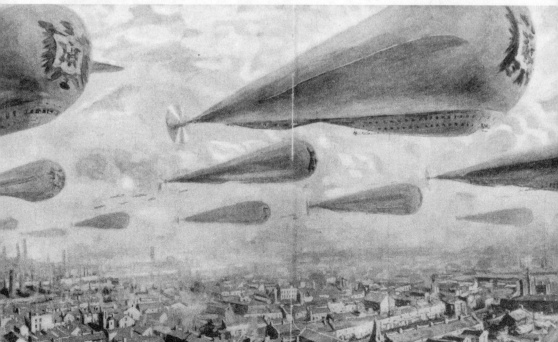

no longer an inaccessible island. It was an ominous development, but one which many had been expecting for some time. The threat from above had preoccupied the popular imagination for several decades already, and in the late nineteenth and early twentieth centuries the public consumed a host of books about future wars and the menace of airships and aeroplanes. Wells himself wrote the most enduring of these in 1908. His *The War in the Air* depicted a catastrophic worldwide conflict fought by roving fleets of airships and aeroplanes. In it, a German airship fleet crosses the Atlantic to launch a devastating raid on New York, bringing the United States to the brink of collapse. In reality, of course, Germany had no such capabilities, at least not yet. But Germany was eager to develop its air potential.

The man whose name was to become synonymous with airships, Graf (Count) Ferdinand von Zeppelin, pioneered the first rigid airship, which he demonstrated on 2 July 1900 at Friedrichshafen on the shore of Lake Constance in Southern Germany. Unlike earlier balloons, LZ1 (*Luftschiff Zeppelin* 1), as it was called, was a streamlined craft with not one single gas bag, but multiple gas cells enclosed within a fabric envelope covering an aluminium frame of girders and rings. Thus, if one or several cells leaked, there would still be enough gas for the 420ft-long airship to remain airborne. In the following years Count Zeppelin developed bigger and better versions of the airship and in 1907 LZ3 was built which was capable of eight hours flight. As such it was capable of travelling much further and longer than any

This illustration from **The War in the Air** *imagines a devastating raid on New York carried out by the German airships. 'As the airships sailed along they smashed up the city as a child will shatter its cities of brick and card. Below, they left ruins and blazing conflagration and heaped and scattered dead... Lower New York was soon a furnace of crimson flames, from which there was no escape.'* **British Library**

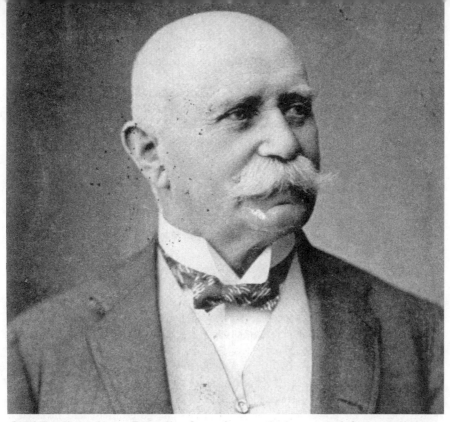

Graf Ferdinand von Zeppelin. One of several pioneers of German lighter-than-air craft, his name would become synonymous with airships in general. Imperial War Museum

aeroplanes of the time, it was more reliable and it could carry passengers or a load. Impressed, the German government funded continued research and development into the Zeppelins and the Army ordered one for themselves, LZ4. This was wrecked in a storm soon after completion, a blow that might have spelled an early end to the airship programme. However, airships had caught the imagination of the German public and such was their support that they contributed six hundred million marks for further development.

More and improved Zeppelins were built and it was now that the German Imperial Navy assumed the airship mantle. Although the Army bought further Zeppelins, it turned to the Schütte-Lanz company for the supply of most of its airships (strictly speaking, only airships built by the Zeppelin company were 'Zeppelins'). The Navy preferred the Zeppelins' use of aluminium to the plywood framework of the Schütte-Lanzs (SLs) and they had the same belief in what airships should do as Count Zeppelin himself. While the Army was content to employ the craft for scouting missions, Count Zeppelin and the Naval Airship Division, formed in 1912, had a more proactive intention: bombing. Their envisaged use of airships was to take war to the enemy; they were to be at the forefront of any offensive in the expected conflict with the Triple Entente, the alliance between Britain, France and Russia.

Setbacks hindered their preparations for war when the Naval Airship Division's first two Zeppelins were destroyed in the autumn of 1913. L1, with *Korvettenkapitän*

Metzing, the first chief of the Naval Airship Division, on board, was lost in the North Sea in September in bad weather; L2, which replaced L1 the day it was lost, caught fire and was destroyed in midair in October. These two disasters claimed the lives of the most skilled and experienced personnel, but they also resulted in the promotion of Peter Strasser to *Korvettenkapitän* and his appointment as Metzing's successor. Strasser was full of passion and energy, and in his new role set about training fresh crews and securing more funds. A convivial man, held in admiration and affection by those under him, he was utterly convinced of the strategic importance of the Zeppelin and instilled this confidence and pride in his men. Despite repeated setbacks in the course of the coming war, Strasser was never to lose his convictions, which ensured that airships would attack Britain throughout the conflict. It is hard to imagine that any other man could have led the Naval Airship Division with such resolve.

Unsurprisingly, German developments caused anxiety in Britain and there were rumours of secret, night-time operations flown by Zeppelins over the country. Alarmed people suspected them of spying on naval facilities and defences, but there were others who dismissed these fears as scare-mongering. One of those vilified as a sensationalist was Lord Northcliffe, the newspaper tycoon. Through the *Daily Mail* he had tried to inspire public interest and concern about aviation, and had offered various air race cash prizes, including £1,000 to the first person to fly across the Channel. Northcliffe attacked the government for what he perceived as complacency about future aerial attack – tragically, he was soon proved right. Britain could not match German air power when the war started. The government had invested a paltry sum in aviation compared not only with the Germans, but also with the French and the United States. Its air power was divided between the Army and the Navy in the form of the Royal Flying Corps and Royal Naval Air Service, which would not combine to form the RAF until April 1918. And, although Britain had its own airships and balloons, these lagged far behind the Germans and were only to perform a scouting role around the coastline, guarding against enemy submarines and fleet movements. Unlike the Zeppelins, British airships had no offensive capability.

No one really knew what to expect from airborne raids in the First World War and there was little preparation for them. There were no shelters or sandbags available early on in the war. There was no standardized warning or all clear signal, police whistles, car horns and bicycle bells being utilized for the purpose, and, from late 1917, boy scout buglers. These all had to be improvised. When war broke out in August 1914 the Admiralty assumed the Home Defence of the capital, the Army the rest of the country. London was defended by a handful of guns that had been modified to fire at a high angle, but none of them were capable of hitting an enemy soaring 10,000ft above; the situation was no better elsewhere in Britain. Those who manned the searchlights and anti-aircraft batteries were often elderly or unfit volunteers, more able men going off to the Front. Lieutenant Commander Alfred Rawlinson of the Royal Naval Volunteer Reserve, the West London Anti-Aircraft Sub-Commander, described Home Defence personnel as 'The deaf, the blind and the mentally deficient'. Whatever their own shortfalls, they were hampered by faulty ammunition and poor equipment. Deficiencies on the ground were matched in the air too. Aeroplanes such as the BE2 and BE8 posed no credible counter to airships

Early improvised air raid warnings in the capital – a horn... Imperial War Museum

...and a tin pan and hammer. Imperial War Museum

– they had neither the altitude, speed nor weapons for the job. Among the ineffective early weapons developed for them to use against airships were petrol bombs trailing fishhooks, designed to catch on to the Zeppelin's envelope. Effective ammunition would not become available for nearly two years.

Alone in the government, Winston Churchill was convinced of the potential air threat. He set about ordering searchlights and calling for airmen at the air base at Hendon to learn how to fly at night. In London, emergency landing grounds were laid out in Regent's Park and Battersea Park, and street lamps were painted black on their tops and sides to reduce visibility from above. Gaps were left in the lighting along certain major roads while open areas were illuminated to confuse raiders, and special constables enforced blacking out lights in homes during the hours of darkness. In his position as First Lord of the Admiralty, Churchill encouraged aeroplanes of the Royal Naval Air Service not to wait for the Zeppelins to come to them, but to carry out pre-emptive strikes, instead. From bases in France, RNAS planes attacked airship sheds at Cologne and Düsseldorf in September and October, the latter resulting in the destruction of the German Army's ZIX by Flight Lieutenant Reginald Marix. The biggest sortie was carried out against Friedrichshafen itself, the birthplace of the Zeppelin and the centre for their design, testing and construction. On 21 November 1914 three Avro 504 biplanes took off from the French aerodrome at Belfort and flew the hundred miles to Lake

Searchlights on Old Lambeth Bridge, London, in 1914. Imperial War Museum

Constance. The returning airmen were awarded Distinguished Service Orders for this ambitious enterprise, but the reality was that despite damaging buildings and a gasworks at Friedrichshafen, none of the Zeppelins under construction were hit. A raid carried out on Christmas Day from seaplane carriers in the North Sea against the Zeppelin bases at Nordholz and Cuxhaven in northern Germany was even more of a fiasco. The British seaplanes were unable to find their targets owing to thick fog and poor maps, and Zeppelins L6 and L5 actually returned the attack by bombing one of the carriers and a British submarine that was rescuing crews from the downed seaplanes – the submarine submerged and was lucky to escape. Notwithstanding the failure, the British press lapped it up as a daring and dramatic adventure; in the *London Gazette* the government was happy to pat itself on the back for a 'successful reconnaissance' of the Heligoland Bight.

Luckily for Britain, Germany had launched no Zeppelin attacks in 1914. Unluckily for Britain, the government was lulled into a false sense of security. Despite nightly reported airship sightings and wild fears of invasion following the shelling of Hartlepool, Scarborough and Whitby by German battle cruisers on 16 December, during the winter of 1914-15 air raid precautions became lax.

CHAPTER 2

The First Zeppelin Raids

*London lay, breathing heavily, oppressed by a nightmare such as the most
ferocious minds of the darkest of the Dark Ages did not dream of.*
Violet Hunt and Ford Madox Hueffer, *Zeppelin Nights*

Athough German airships were slow to attack Britain, they were involved in the war
from the beginning, largely fulfilling a reconnaissance role with those of the Navy
over the North Sea and those of the Army over the land fronts. Unhappily for the
Army, they lost three SLs in the first week of the war on the Western Front, when
they flew too low and were hit by ground fire; the same befell one in the east. This
allowed Strasser's naval airships to take the lead in the race to be the first to bomb
Britain. The German public and Naval High Command were eager to begin the
assault as soon as possible and plans were made to bomb London, but the Kaiser
prevaricated, worried about the effect this unprecedented form of warfare might
have on the opinion of neutral countries such as the United States. Believing, along
with many others, that the war would be quickly over, he thought strategic bombing
would be unnecessary. Such political niceties prevented the airships from taking the

*The control car of a German Navy Zeppelin, with the front to the left. Note,
silhouetted in a window halfway along the gondola, a crew member beside
a machine gun.* Imperial War Museum

Inside a Zeppelin control car: the electric bomb switches. Imperial War Museum

opportunity to strike while British defences were at their weakest, with neither AA (nicknamed 'Archie' by the British) nor planes capable of intercepting them.

As the war lengthened the Kaiser came under mounting military and public pressure, especially after three German civilians were killed in a French aeroplane raid on Freiburg, and on 10 January 1915 he finally gave qualified approval for the aerial bombardment of Britain. Damage to Royal Palaces and historic buildings was forbidden and, in a futile effort to avoid civilian casualties, it was ordered that only military targets such as coastal defences and the London Docks were to be bombed – futile because accurate bombing was not technologically possible and because targets such as the Docks were located within densely populated areas. Strasser, however, was under no illusion that a distinction could be made between civilian and military targets, nor did he have any reservations. Six Zeppelins were immediately made available: L3, L4, L5, L6, L7 and L8. Great expectations were had of the airships, expressed in Germany in a popular song at the time:

> *Zeppelin, flieg,*
> *Hilf ums in Krieg,*
> *Fliege nach England,*
> *England wird abgebrannt,*
> *Zeppelin, flieg!*

An English translation of which is:

> *Zeppelin, fly,*
> *Help us in the War,*
> *Fly to England,*
> *England shall be destroyed by fire,*
> *Zeppelin, fly!*

16

The Zeppelin crews on whom these hopes depended were among the most highly motivated personnel in the German services. They were all volunteers and a sense of comradeship existed between the officers and NCOs that was not found anywhere else. Airship commanders knew their crews personally, as well as the ground crews of fitters and cleaners. These latter, termed 'the ground acrobats', were hard-working and versatile and formed a ready pool of new aircrew members. The crew on any one airship varied according to its mission – particularly heavy bomb payloads would require the minimal possible to offset the weight – but they generally numbered eighteen. These consisted of a captain, an executive officer, two warrant officers, some five or more petty officers and ten machinists. Command and control of the ship was situated in the forward gondola or car, into which the captain, executive officer, navigator and two petty officers attending the rudder and elevation controls would be crammed. In a soundproof compartment behind them sat two petty officer wireless operators, tuning in to wireless stations on the German and Belgium coasts in order to determine their location – an unreliable method and one the British could pick up and overhear. The engineer and his machinists were positioned in the engine gondola; the sailmaker, who maintained the envelope and gas cells, was under the keel.

To protect against the sub-zero temperatures at high altitudes the crew wore thick woollen underwear, their blue naval uniforms, leather overalls, fur overcoats, scarves, goggles, leather helmets and thick gloves of leather and wool. When outside of the gondolas large felt overshoes were donned over their ordinary shoes. Even in the height of summer the temperature on board an airship could fall as low as 25°-30°C below zero. To combat altitude sickness (anoxia) resulting from the thin air, bottles of liquid oxygen (later liquid air, which was more palatable and had fewer side effects) were carried round the neck: these were breathed through mouthpieces and pipes resembling hookahs. Zeppelin crews were well rationed on their voyages with thermos flasks full of strong coffee, bread, chocolate, sausages and tins of stew that were chemically heated on opening – cooking was not allowed of course – a state of affairs that continued even towards the end of the war when Germany suffered crippling food shortages. They also received flasks of rum or brandy that they were not allowed to drink unless the airship reached a certain height, though they often drank them anyway and then refilled the flasks with water if the commander recalled them. Although parachutes were available, Zeppelin crews generally discarded them in their effort to carry the least weight; also, parachutes were seen as useless over the sea and it was doubted whether they could be employed in time in a crisis, for when an airship caught fire the blaze was furious and spread rapidly.

Airship defences comprised Maxim machine guns that could be deployed in the gondolas and on the top platform (reached by a ladder through the middle of the ship), but again concern to keep weight to a minimum meant that these were often dispensed with, the ability to climb higher than anti-aircraft fire or hostile aircraft being a better defence than bullets. In case of a close call, however, dummy machine guns were sometimes mounted to deter the enemy – the trigger operating an electric flash in the muzzle to simulate firing. In action, silence and darkness were maintained on board, the only illumination coming from a radium coating to the instruments.

*On duty with the German High Seas Fleet in the North Sea. A photograph taken from L54 of the battleship SMS **Markgraf.*** Imperial War Museum

From a neutral perspective there is much to admire about the men who worked in such harsh conditions and endured tense hours over enemy territory, straining their eyes for hostile aircraft. When not on raids and being shot at – most of their time was in fact spent on reconnaissance duty over the North Sea on behalf of the German High Seas Fleet – their fragile, flammable craft were vulnerable to bad weather, especially thunderstorms which could ignite an airship in mid-air, and mechanical problems. Even moving about an airship was fraught with danger. Movement between the gondolas was via a narrow catwalk running along the keel, and to reach this one had to negotiate a thirteen-rung ladder, an especially hard task in strong winds or frost, or when dizzy from the altitude. As a result, a number of men were lost by falling overboard. No wonder some airshipmen thought the German public underestimated the risks they faced.

The first airship raid unleashed on Britain set off from Fuhlsbüttel and Nordholz on 19 January 1915. Zeppelins L3 and L4, captained by *Kapitänleutnants* Hans Fritz and Count Magnus von Platen-Hallermund, planned to attack the Humber; L6, commanded by *Oberleutnant zur See* Horst von Buttlar, with Strasser accompanying him, had the more prestigious target of London. However, rain, snow and poor visibility led L3 and L4 off course over Norfolk, while engine failure forced L6 to retire home early, not even having reached England. Britain's first ever air raid casualties were inflicted that night in Great Yarmouth by Fritz in L3. He arrived over the coastal town at 8.30 pm and dropped a number of high explosives and incendiary bombs from 5,000ft. One of these landed close to the town centre in

18

Damage caused to St Peter's House, Great Yarmouth, by Kapitänleutnant
*Hans Fritz in naval Zeppelin L3, on 19 January 1915. Outside, in St Peter's
Plain, a bomb killed Martha Taylor and Samuel Smith. They were Britain's
first air raid victims.* Imperial War Museum

St Peter's Plain killing Samuel Smith, a fifty-three-year-old cobbler, and Martha
Taylor, a seventy-two-year-old spinster. Mr Smith had just come outside from his
workshop to investigate the noise of the Zeppelin's engines, while Miss Taylor was
returning home from the grocers. Three others were injured in Great Yarmouth that
night. At King's Lynn L4 was the cause of two deaths from shock and thirteen injured.

The next day the national newspapers kicked up a fuss about this example of
German 'frightfulness', denouncing it as murderous and cowardly. At the same time
they downplayed the military significance of the raid. It was described as having
been no worse than a traffic accident or a gas explosion, and Francis Perrot wrote in
the *Manchester Guardian* that people were even 'pleasantly excited' by the raid. This

was not quite true. Many of Great Yarmouth's inhabitants were upset, especially the day after the raid when they could see the damage that had been caused. They were incensed that no warning was issued prior to the attack and that the town's authorities had extinguished the streetlights only after L3 had already departed. There was also disappointment that British aircraft did not engage the enemy airships. In Germany, despite the failure of the raid overall, there was satisfaction that bombing had at least begun. The crews of L3 and L4 were decorated with the Iron Cross and newspapers excitedly reported the air raids as offering the best means of shortening the war. As expected, neutral countries condemned the attack, including Denmark, Holland, Norway, Sweden, Switzerland and the United States. Ignoring their protests, the Kaiser bowed to pressure from the Naval High Command and on 12 February authorized attacks against war material and military establishments of every kind, as well as fuel depots and docks. Abortive and ineffectual raids continued during the next few months, with commanders, including Strasser, claiming to have hit their targets and come under attack to cover their failure. Bombs meant for the Humber and Newcastle fell on Lowestoft and in fields near Tynemouth.

Chief Constable Charles Hunt examines part of a bomb dropped during the raid on King's Lynn. Imperial War Museum

In mid-1915 the Army and Navy took receipt of larger, more powerful airships, over $1,000,000\text{ft}^3$ in capacity, 536ft in length, 61ft in diameter and capable of 55mph powered by four 210hp Maybach engines, which enabled the airships to climb at over 1,000ft a minute. To the chagrin of the Navy it was to be one of the Army's airships that would be first to bomb London. On the clear evening of 31 May 1915 LZ38, commanded by *Hauptmann* Erich Linnarz, set off from Brussels with thirty-five explosive bombs and ninety incendiary devices. Flying over Margate and Southend, he appeared over north-east London, which was well lit. At ten to eleven Linnarz dropped his initial bombs over the East End and saw flames and smoke rise beneath him. Because of his height, Linnarz was barely visible and could hardly be heard as he released his ton of bombs. AA proved ineffective, none of the nine aeroplanes sent up to locate him in the night sky was able to find him and one crashed, killing its pilot. Below, the scene was one of horror and panic. Although the family living at 16 Alkham Road, Stoke Newington, where the very first bomb fell, managed to escape the ensuing conflagration, a fire in nearby Cowper Street claimed the life of three-year-old Elsie Leggatt and her sister, May. More deaths followed.

The total number of casualties in the raid was relatively low – seven were killed, including four children, and thirty-five were wounded – but Londoners were furious. Their resentment was intensified by the findings of a public inquest into the deaths of two of the raid's victims, Henry and Caroline Good of Balls Pond Road, Dalston, whose charred bodies had been discovered by a policeman the morning after the raid. They were found kneeling by their bedside, their clothes burnt off them and Mr Good's arm clasped about his wife's waist: it seemed they had died while they were at prayer, overcome by smoke and then flames. The ill feelings caused by these lurid details led to outbreaks of violence, and in the aftermath of the raid anyone with a German-sounding name or suspected of German descent who was not already interned risked attack and their homes or business premises being destroyed by mobs. Meanwhile, thousands paid a penny each to wander through the devastated houses where some of the victims had perished.

A week after Linnarz's foray, on the night of 6/7 June, the German Army launched another raid, by three airships, LZ37, LZ38 and LZ39. This time the raid was abortive and LZ37, commanded by *Oberleutnant zur See* von der Haegen, fell prey

Flight Sub-Lieutenant Reginald Warneford, RNAS, who destroyed German Army Zeppelin LZ37 on 7 June 1915. Awarded the Victoria Cross and **Legion d'Honneur,** *he died in a flying accident on 17 June.* Imperial War Museum

to a British pilot as it came back from a foggy Channel. Flight Sub-Lieutenant Reginald A. J. Warneford, RNAS, whose flight was based at Furnes in Belgium, intercepted the Zeppelin around 2.00 am near Ghent and managed to climb above it despite stiff machine-gun fire from the airship's five Maxims. Over Bruges, as LZ37 began a descent for the airbase at Melle-Gontrode, Warneford dived from 10,000ft and released the six 20lb bombs from the fuselage of his Morane-Saulnier monoplane. The last bomb was a hit and the Zeppelin exploded. The burning wreckage fell 8,000ft on the Convent of St Elizabeth in Bruges, killing two nuns along with a child and a man. The burnt bodies and limbs of the airship crew were scattered over the convent, but one crew member had a miraculous escape. A hundred feet before the Zeppelin crashed, *Steuermann* Alfred Mühler was thrown in flames from the forward gondola and fell through an attic skylight on to a nun's empty feather bed. (He made a full recovery.) Warneford in the meantime was fighting for control of his aeroplane, which had been turned over by the blast and released gases from the Zeppelin. He regained control, but was forced down in a field behind the enemy line because of damage to his petrol supply. Instead of destroying his aeroplane and waiting to be captured, he repaired the machine and started its engine on his own, getting away just as German cavalrymen arrived on the scene. It was the first success against the raiders and it was duly celebrated. The next day Warneford received a personal telegram from the King and was awarded the Victoria Cross. His glory was to be short-lived, however. Less than a fortnight later, on 17 June, he was flying in a Henry Farman biplane when its tail fell off and crashed near Paris. Warneford and his passenger, an American journalist, were both killed.

In addition to Warneford's destruction of LZ37, the German Army also lost the returned LZ38 in the early hours of 7 June, when Flight Lieutenant John Philip Wilson and Flight Sub-Lieutenant John Stanley Mills, RNAS, bombed the airship sheds at Brussels-Evère. This loss of two Zeppelins in one night led the German Army largely to abandon their airship raids on Britain and plan other means of attack. The loss did not discourage the Naval Airship Division, however. The Navy

The Morane-Saulnier monoplane with which Warneford successfully bombed LZ37. Imperial War Museum

Devastation in Hull: Market Place, beside Holy Trinity Church. **Kapitänleutnant** *Heinrich Mathy, in L9, attacked the city during the night of 6/7 June 1915.* Hull Museums

in fact had made a successful sortie the same night as the failed Army attack, when the lone L9 managed to locate Hull shortly after midnight. Commanded by *Kapitänleutnant* Heinrich Mathy, the most daring and able of Germany's airship captains, L9 dropped over a dozen explosives and more than forty incendiaries before heading for Grimsby and then home. Twenty-four died in the raid and twice that many were injured. The dock area suffered the worst damage and, as in London, after the raid was over there was rioting against the premises of small shopkeepers with Germanic names. For many nights after this, citizens of Hull abandoned their

Naval Zeppelin L9, which **Kapitänleutnant** *Mathy commanded during the raid on Hull, 6/7 June 1915.* Imperial War Museum

homes in the town for the safety of the surrounding countryside. The Naval Airship Division followed up its Hull raid just over a week later on 15/16 June, with one against Tyneside and the Jarrow dockyards. L10 (*Kapitänleutnant* Klaus Hirsch) arrived over the Northumberland coast at 12.25 am and found the target conveniently illuminated by the industrial lighting of the night shift. Eighteen deaths and seventy-two injured was the result, as well as resentment that there was no protection from the raid and that no warning was provided. Only the short summer nights spared Britain any more raids in the next two months.

When the offensive was renewed in August the objectives were London and the Humber area. These were only half-successful, but in September the raids intensified. On 8/9 September *Kapitänleutnant* Mathy, commanding L13, bombed Golders Green and central London, including Bloomsbury, Holborn and the City. He inflicted a massive amount of damage and dropped the single biggest bomb yet, weighing 300kg (660lb), on Bartholomew Close, north of Newgate Street. From his view up above, Mathy was delighted with its result, writing in his report:

> *The explosive effect of the 300kg bomb must be very great, since a whole row of lights vanished in one stroke.*

Rather cheekily, he also dropped a ham-bone attached to a parachute over Barnet: on it was painted the German flag, the words '*Zum Andeken an das ausgehungerte Deutschland*' ('A memento from starved-out Germany'), and a drawing of a Zeppelin bombing 'Edward Grey', the British foreign minister, with the inscription, '*Was fang ich, armer Teufel, an?*' ('What shall I, poor devil, do?'). Less amusingly, twenty-six died in the raid and ninety-four were injured. Although the capital's anti-aircraft

More ruin at the hands of Mathy, this time in the City of London. Buildings in Oat Lane, Wood Street, gutted during the raid of 8/9 September 1915, which, in material terms, was the most destructive of the entire war. Imperial War Museum

guns forced Mathy to rise above the clouds at 11,000ft and out of sight of the millions of watching Londoners, there was disbelief that on such an otherwise calm, clear night when the Zeppelin could be plainly seen it had not been spotted *before* its arrival over London. None of the Home Defence squadron aeroplanes had been able to find it and the observation posts had failed completely. A few days after the raid the retired Admiral Sir Percy Scott was put in charge of London's defences. He scrambled together extra guns while discarding the ineffectual 1-pounder 'pom poms', organized mobile AA on lorry chassis, and requested on loan from France one of their latest 75mm AA auto-cannons. These were mounted on armoured cars and had proved valuable in the defence of Paris. Scott wanted a sample so that British copies could be produced, but his plan was retarded by the Admiralty's slowness in writing an official letter to the French War Ministry. When nearly a week had passed by without anything being done, Scott despatched his assistant, Lieutenant Commander Rawlinson, to bring back one of the guns, letter or no letter. Rawlinson fulfilled his mission and duly returned to England, parking the mobile French gun with ironic relish on Horse Guards Parade, right outside the Admiralty offices, which even now had yet to pen their missive.

The newly arrived gun, the only one in London capable of firing high explosive AA shells, was soon put to the test. On the night of 13/14 October Zeppelins L11, L14, L15, L16, and Mathy in L13 again, converged for a combined raid against London. L11 turned back from the coast and the only Zeppelin to arrive over the centre of the capital was L15, commanded by *Kapitänleutnant* Joachim Breithaupt, at 9.30 pm, where it was greeted by intense anti-aircraft fire. Rawlinson's own account of the night's defences provides us with an idea of how much or how little the German airmen were up against and reads like a farce. Earlier in the evening he and the crew manning the French gun were ordered to proceed from their Armoured Car Headquarters in Ladbroke Grove to the Artillery Ground in the City. After waiting agonizing minutes while his men turned up late, his convoy got underway with headlights glaring and sirens wailing only to run into the dense traffic of the West End. He tells us:

> At that time there was no system of 'air raid warnings', 'raid shelters', or 'maroons', such as was organized later on, and the streets on this occasion were crammed both with vehicular traffic and pedestrians. Everyone understood at once, in the light of their experience during the previous month, the moment they saw us coming, that an air raid was imminent. They did not, however, know 'where to go' or 'what to do' though none of them had any doubt at all that the most pressing and most vital thing they had to do was TO GET OUT OF OUR WAY.

> I feel quite confident that no man who took that drive will ever forget any part of it, and particularly Oxford Street, which presented an almost unbelievable spectacle. I had such an anxious job myself that I had no time to laugh, but I am sure I 'smiled' all the way. After passing the Marble Arch the traffic in Oxford Street became much thicker. The noise of our 'sirens' being as 'deafening' as the glare of our 'headlights' was 'dazzling,' the omnibuses in every direction were seeking safety on the pavement. I also observed, out of the corner of my eye, several instances of people flattening themselves against the shop windows, the public at that time being infinitely more fearful of a gun moving at such a terrific speed than they were of any German bombs, of whose possibilities they had then but little experience.

After negotiating the evening crowds of Oxford Street in record time, Rawlinson drove straight through road works at Holborn before arriving at the Artillery Ground. There the mobile 75mm fired on L15; though they failed to hit the Zeppelin, they came close and justifiably claimed to have driven him away. Tragically, it was too late for some. As Londoners packed the streets to watch the raid, L15 had dropped a series of high explosives and incendiaries aimed at the Admiralty next to Trafalgar Square. Owing to the forward momentum of the Zeppelin, these fell half a mile off target along the congested Strand and Aldwych. Theatres were hit, inducing panic, and an omnibus was blown up, killing the driver and conductor and a special constable as he was stepping off. Further bombs from L15 rained down on the Inns of Court. Other Zeppelins that night bombed Woolwich, where the Arsenal had an incredible escape, and Croydon in the suburbs, as well as Hythe and Tunbridge Wells to the south, and Hertford to the north of London. A total of seventy-one were killed and nearly 130 were injured. For the Germans, the night was a success, even though they had failed to concentrate collective firepower against central London because of communication problems between the airships.

The next significant raid occurred early in 1916. On 31 January nine Zeppelins flew from Germany and bombed various places in the Midlands, including Derby, Burton upon Trent and the suburbs of Birmingham, leaving in their wake seventy dead and 113 injured. Several of the airship commanders afterwards claimed to have bombed Liverpool, which was their intended target, but none of them actually had. This was partly attributable to the airships' usual poor navigation owing to weather, height and the general inability to discern the ground at night. The compass freezing at high altitude contributed to the problem and the ineffectual radio direction-finding stations on the North Sea coast that the Germans used did not relieve it. However, it also appears that the captains' reports of success were intentionally exaggerated to justify the continuing Zeppelin campaign. Strasser, aboard L11,

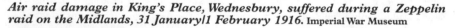

Air raid damage in King's Place, Wednesbury, suffered during a Zeppelin raid on the Midlands, 31 January/1 February 1916. Imperial War Museum

commanded by von Buttlar, was a party to this deceit, but it does seem that he was honourable enough not to drop any bombs in the several hours L11 was over England because he failed to find a military target. The most noteworthy incident of the raid occurred as the airships made their way home. L19, commanded by *Kapitänleutnant* Odo Loewe, was fired at by Dutch riflemen over the Friesian Islands and suffered engine trouble, eventually coming down in the North Sea. The crew could have been saved when a British trawler, *King Stephen*, came across them at seven in the morning, but the vessel's skipper refused to pick them up, fearing his crew of nine would have been overpowered by the Zeppelin's sixteen. The airmen were left to their fate and all drowned in the next few days, but not before writing bitter farewell messages in bottles which were afterwards washed ashore to tell their story. In Britain there was little sympathy for the forsaken airmen, but German public opinion was outraged at this perceived breach of the Geneva Convention and their newspapers denounced 'the brutality of the British character'.

Considering the huge number of bombs and incendiaries dropped by the raiders, the number of casualties was relatively light. What was most alarming was the poor defensive showing against the Zeppelins who roamed at will for as long as twelve hours. Also, six Home Defence aeroplanes were destroyed due to pilot error and mechanical failure, and two squadron commanders lost their lives. There was still no effective defence against the airships, despite the best endeavours of crackpot inventors who bombarded the War Ministry's Aeronautics Committee with such

Cartoon from **Punch**, *March 1915.* **Punch Publications**

WHAT THE WAR OFFICE HAS TO PUT UP WITH FROM INVENTORS.
1. THE BOMB-CATCHER.

Naval Airship Division Zeppelins setting off for a raid in 1915, including L10, L11, L12 and L13. Imperial War Museum

proposals as aerial mines and heat rays. A better early warning system was created with a central control room at Horse Guards in Whitehall relaying information to Warning Controllers in the regions, who would then pass it on to the police, factories and others. But there were still no planes available that could ascend as high as the Zeppelins and the Home Defence squadrons would not be amalgamated into one until May when No. 39 Squadron, RFC, was formed, with its HQ first at Hounslow, then at Woodford in Essex. Although some detachments covered Newcastle, Sheffield and Birmingham, until the summer England north of London was open to the raiders. Too few guns were yet capable of hurting the Zeppelins and the best that could be hoped was that anti-aircraft fire would force the airships higher and make their targeting less effective. The German aircrews were undeterred.

They duly returned on 5/6 March, three Zeppelins setting out in appalling weather for Rosyth, Tyneside and Middlesbrough. Blown off course, L11 and L14 managed, in spite of snowstorms, to locate Hull as an alternative and inflicted further damage and misery around the docks. *Korvettenkapitän* Viktor Schütze in L11 waited for the clouds above the Humber city to drift away before beginning his attack. He reported:

> *The town, though very well darkened, showed up clearly under the starlit sky like a drawing, with streets, blocks of houses, quays and dock basins beneath the airship... During a period of twenty minutes incendiary and high explosive bombs were dropped on the harbour and docks... The first H.E. bomb struck the quay, big portions of which went up, and another hit the lock-gate of one of the harbour basins. The burst was so directly on the gate that it might have been taken for a gun fired off there. Buildings collapsed like houses of cards. One hit had an especially far-reaching effect: radiating round the burst more and more houses collapsed and finally showed up, in the snow-covered area, as a black and gigantic hole... With binoculars it was possible to see people running hither and thither in the glare of the fires.*

There was no AA defence against Schütze and the other Zeppelin, and a gun mounted on the roof of an engineering works was discovered to be merely a dummy, set up to reassure locals after the first raid nine months previously. Angry residents were left to mourn eighteen dead and tend fifty-two injured.

Britain seemed incapable of defending itself. But in the following weeks and months some luck would go its way and a new weapon would be introduced into the fray.

CHAPTER 3

The Zeppelin's Falter

*Talking of cheering, they say it was wonderful to hear all London Cheering –
people who have heard thousands of huge crowds cheering before say they
have heard nothing like it… It swelled and sank, first one quarter of London,
then another. Thousands, one might say millions of throats giving vent to
thousands of feelings.*
Lieutenant William Leefe Robinson VC, RFC
Letter to his parents following the destruction of SL11.

On 31 March 1916 ten Zeppelins – seven Navy, three
Army – set out to raid London, but four abandoned
the mission because of the weather and mechanical
problems and the others again ended up off course.
They dropped their loads on towns in the eastern
counties instead of the capital. Mathy in L13 suffered
anti-aircraft hits near Stowmarket in Suffolk,
damaging two of his craft's gas cells. He was lucky to
return home. L15, under *Kapitänleutnant* Joachim
Breithaupt, was not so fortunate. While over the
Thames at 10.00 pm, the Zeppelin was hit by a gun
from Purfleet, Essex, rupturing four gas cells. As
Breithaupt struggled in vain to gain height, Second
Lieutenant Alfred de Bathe Brandon, RFC, attacked
the Zeppelin in his BE2c, dropping Ranken darts and
incendiary bombs. He failed to hit it, but L15 slowly
came down anyway, in the sea off Margate, despite
the best efforts of its crew who jettisoned everything
to keep it airborne – bombs, guns, surplus fuel, even
the secret papers and wireless. Although one crew

**Second Lieutenant Alfred de Bathe Brandon,
RFC, who attacked Zeppelin L15 over the
Thames Estuary, 31 March/1 April 1916.**
Imperial War Museum

**L15 after it came down in the sea off Margate, 1 April 1916. It sank before
it could be towed into harbour.** Imperial War Museum

member was drowned, the others were rescued and captured. No one at the time was sure who was precisely responsible for the downing of L15 so the Lord Mayor of London's offer of £500 for the first Zeppelin to be brought down was replaced with commemorative medals distributed to all the gun crews involved. As the first success scored by the Home Defence, the event was of immense relief to Britons, although some disbelieved the news when they first heard it. One, Miss Viola Bawtree, recorded:

> Great rejoicings. I saw the news first, on my way home from Sutton. The headlines on a poster, 'The Raid. Zeppelin Brought Down. Official.' I smiled half sceptically, too good to be true – our guns couldn't do such a thing. Then I met Dr. Rice, reading a newspaper. He told me it was really true and I hurried home to tell the glad news. It's such extra good news to know that a gun can hit a Zeppelin. We've been so disappointed in the guns when we found that they were apparently only to keep the raiders from coming low, and that we mustn't expect them ever to hit enough to do damage.

Though she added:

> Perhaps the Zeppelin crew was extra brave and was flying low, to aim their bombs better.

Ineffective raids by the German Navy and Army followed in the next few days and months, targets including Sunderland, Leith, Edinburgh and London. Strasser succeeding in maintaining belief in the potential of the airships though, and he had only a short while to wait before the 'super Zeppelins' would be available. The L20 class of airship was already ready for deployment – Zeppelins which were over 1,250,000ft³, were 585ft 5in. in length and

A dejected looking **Kapitänleutnant** *Breithaupt,* *the captured commander of* *L15.* **For his bombing of** *London on 13 October the* *previous year the Kaiser had* *awarded him the* **Pour le** **Mérite.** Imperial War Museum

61ft 4in. in diameter, and had four 260hp Maybach HSLu engines giving them a speed of up to 60mph. Inauspiciously, on 2 May L20 was wrecked when it came down in a Norwegian fjord after losing its way over Scotland, while L7 was shot down by British cruisers when its fuel tank was ruptured while scouting for the German Navy during the Royal Navy's attempted seaplane attack on the Zeppelin sheds at Tondern. But in August three 'super Zeppelins' were ready – L30, L31 and L32. These were more streamlined than the earlier airships and measured almost 2,000,000ft³, were 649ft 7in long and 78ft 5in in diameter. Driven by six 240hp Maybach HSLu engines, they were capable of 60mph and had a ceiling of 17,400ft unloaded. With their advent, Strasser confidently predicted that Zeppelins would win the war for Germany.

The first raid involving one of these was set for the night of 2/3 September against London. L32, commanded by *Oberleutnant zur See* Werner Peterson, and eleven other naval airships combined for a massive attack, and four Army airships were to attack separately at the same time. One Army and one Navy airship each turned back early, but this was still to be the largest airship raid on Britain in the war. Confident of success, however, the Germans were completely unaware that the British airmen they were to face were in receipt of a newly developed secret weapon they were very keen to try out: the incendiary bullet. The Home Defence squadrons had been issued with Brock-Pomeroy-Buckingham ammunition, a mix of explosive and phosphorous bullets intended to release and then ignite the airships' hydrogen gas cells. This was to be used with great effect by nineteen-year-old Lieutenant William Leefe Robinson, of No. 39 Squadron, RFC. He had taken off in his BE2c from Suttons Farm airfield and been flying for three hours when he intercepted Army airship SL11, a Schütte-Lanz type commanded by England-born *Hauptmann* Wilhelm Schramm, after another Army airship LZ98 had earlier evaded him by climbing out of his reach. SL11 had approached central London from Tottenham and Finsbury in the north-east, but had been forced to retreat by AA, and was caught by Robinson after searchlights picked it up just after 2.00 am. Robinson described what followed in his report to his Commanding Officer:

> *I saw shells bursting and night tracer shells flying around it. When I drew closer I noticed that the anti-aircraft aim was too high or too low; also a good many some 800 feet behind – a few tracers went right over. I could hear the bursts when about 3,000 feet from the Zeppelin. I flew about 800 feet below it from bow to stern and distributed one drum along it (alternate New Brock and Pomeroy). It seemed to have no effect; I therefore moved to one side and gave it another drum distributed along its side – without apparent effect. I then got behind it (by this time I was very close – 500 feet or less below) and concentrated one drum on one part (underneath rear). I was then*

German Army airship SL11, falls in flames at Cuffley, 3 September 1916. A photograph taken from Walthamstow in north-east London. Imperial War Museum

at a height of 11,500 feet when attacking Zeppelin. I hardly finished the drum before I saw the part fired at glow. In a few seconds the whole rear part was blazing. When the third drum was fired there were no searchlights on the Zeppelin and no anti-aircraft was firing. I quickly got out of the way of the falling blazing Zeppelin and being very excited fired off a few red Very's lights and dropped a parachute flare.

Millions witnessed the destruction of SL11, which could be seen from thirty-five miles away. One of them was Muriel Dayrell-Browning, staying at the Strathmore Hotel in Tavistock Square, central London. She captured the exhilarating event in a letter to her mother 'about The Raid last night – the Sight of my Life!':

At 2.30 I was awakened by a terrific explosion and was at the window in one bound when another deafening one shook the house. Nearly above us sailed a cigar of bright silver in the full glare of about 20 magnificent searchlights. A few lights roamed around trying to pick out his companion. Our guns made a deafening row and shells burst all around her. For some extraordinary reason she was dropping no bombs. The night was absolutely still with a few splendid stars. It was a magnificent sight and the whole of London was looking on holding its breath.

She continued watching the spectacle, perched on the window ledge and in her dressing gown, while the rest of the household was escorted to the cellar for safety – some were, reasonably, more frightened than excited. The airship disappeared northwards into cloud and she 'thought the fun was over':

Then – from the direction of Barnet and very high a brilliant red light appeared... Then we saw it was the Zep diving head first. That was a sight. She dived slowly at first as only the foremost ballonet was on fire. Then the second burst and the flames tore up into the sky and then the thud and cheers thundered all round us from every direction. The plane lit up all London and was rose red. Those deaths must be the most dramatic in the world's history. They fell – a cone of blazing wreckage thousands of feet – watched by 8 millions of their enemies.
It was magnificent, the most thrilling scene imaginable.

People gazing from the rooftops and streets clapped and cheered the fiery spectacle, others broke into spontaneous renditions of the national anthem to the accompaniment of engine whistles and factory hooters. The airship came down in Hertfordshire at the village of Cuffley. Staying there on holiday was schoolboy Patrick Blundstone, who watched SL11 crash a mere hundred yards away, in a field opposite his house. He conveyed the grisly scene in a letter to his father:

I would rather not describe the condition of the crew, of course they were dead – burnt to death. They were roasted, there is absolutely no other word for it. They were brown, like the outside of Roast Beef. One had his legs off at the knees, and you could see the joint!

The next day, a Sunday, tens of thousands of visitors came to view the smoking wreckage and collect pieces of twisted wire and charred wood as souvenirs. In the week the perished crew were buried with full military honours in a ceremony at nearby Potters Bar. Many, regarding them as murderers, resented this – the vicar of Cuffley church had refused them burial at all – and a woman hurled eggs at their coffins. There were others, however, who acknowledged the bravery of the aircrew and did not begrudge them this dignity. Robinson, meanwhile, had become a

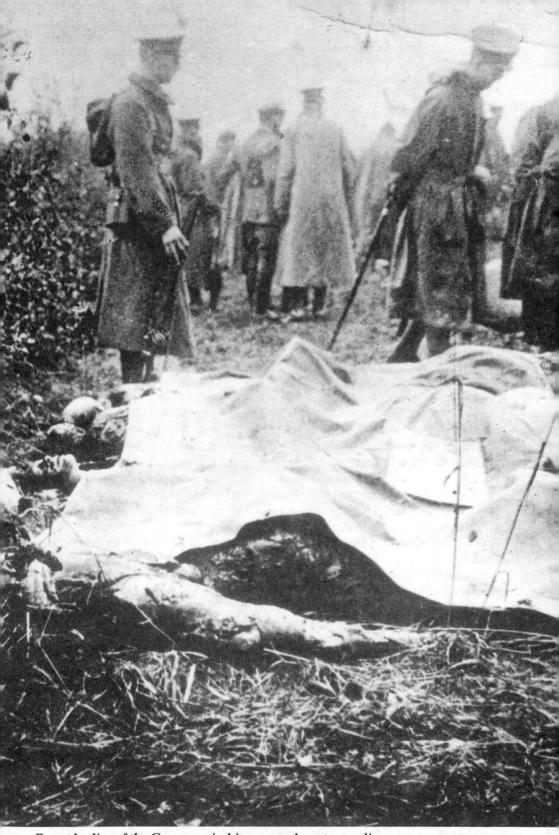

Burnt bodies of the German airshipmen under a tarpaulin cover. Imperial War Museum

Lieutenant William Leefe Robinson, RFC, leaving Windsor Castle after his investiture with the Victoria Cross. Imperial War Museum

national hero and was awarded the Victoria Cross, the only one presented for an action in Britain. He was inundated with interviews and invitations, and received prize money totalling £4,200, a huge sum at the time. Paintings of the burning airship were sent to him along with other tokens of gratitude, poems were dedicated to him and babies, flowers and hats were named after him. His photograph in the newspapers made him recognized everywhere he went. Unfortunately, Robinson's enjoyment of his triumph and fame was cut short in April next year when he was shot down in France by a German flight led by the 'Red Baron', Manfred von Richtofen. Captured, Robinson survived as a prisoner of war but, weakened by his brutal imprisonment, he succumbed to the influenza epidemic after he returned home in December 1918. Still, his feat in 1916 had come at an important time, cheering the country after the disappointments of the Somme and the loss of Secretary of War, Lord Kitchener. The victory against SL11 also gave a welcome boost of morale to the other Home Defence pilots who were doing their best in trying circumstances. They enjoyed little of the kudos attached to aerial combat over the Western Front where the Commander-in-Chief, General Sir Douglas Haig, hoarded most of the better aeroplanes, yet they had to go up on patrol in all weathers when the alarm sounded, and unlike their airship adversaries they were open to the elements. They risked life and limb flying at night amid 'friendly' AA. They had no on board illumination, nor proper landing lights, which made take-off and landing an extremely hazardous operation, and claimed the lives of a number of pilots.

The raid of 2/3 September was the most ambitious that the Germans had yet made and had proved a failure. When the other airships had seen the downfall of SL11 they quickly released their remaining bombs and made their separate ways home. Despite dropping 263 bombs and 200 incendiary devices, only four people were killed and sixteen hurt. The German Army would never use airships to raid

Britain again and henceforth restricted its Airship Service to reconnaissance duties, until wound up in the summer of 1917, some of the crews transferring to the Navy. The Naval Airship Division was demoralized and their pride dented, but Strasser remained convinced that airships still had a vital role to play against Britain. Another heavy raid was planned within the month to make up for the last one, but this was to prove even more disastrous. On 23/24 September twelve airships attacked Britain, including three 'super Zeppelins'. L31, under *Kapitänleutnant* Mathy, the leader of the raid, came up through Kent and Surrey under the cover of cloud and attacked south London, bombing Streatham, Brixton and Kennington. Magnesium parachute flares released by Mathy dazzled the eyes of the gun crews and observers on the ground, and neither searchlights nor AA could locate him. Crossing London, he deposited the remainder of his bombs on Leyton, bringing his night's tally to twenty-two killed and seventy-five wounded. L31 escaped northwards via Great Yarmouth, but others of the Zeppelins were not so lucky. Just after midnight L33 (*Kapitänleutnant der Reserve* Alois Böcker) dropped a number of bombs and incendiaries over the East End, destroying residential buildings, offices and factories and causing large-scale fires in which eleven died, but was hit by an anti-aircraft shell, which ruptured one of its cells. Everything possible was thrown overboard in order to keep it aloft, but L33 had lost too much gas and an hour later landed in a field at Little Wigborough, near Mersea Island, in Essex. Although its back was broken the Zeppelin was recovered virtually intact – the crew had been unable to scuttle it with flares because too little hydrogen remained.

A house near Streatham Hill Station, south London, used as a girls' school until shortly before it was bombed by **Kapitänleutnant** *Mathy during the raid of 23/24 September 1916.* **Imperial War Museum**

The structural remains of L33, at Little Wigborough in Essex. It was forced down on 24 September 1916; Kapitänleutnant der Reserve Alois Böcker and his crew were taken prisoner. Imperial War Museum

The officers and men of L32 under *Oberleutnant zur See* Peterson fared worse. Caught in searchlight beams at 12.45 am, Second Lieutenant Frederick Sowrey of No. 39 Squadron stole up on the Zeppelin in his BE2c and distributed two drums of incendiary bullets along its underside without effect, the Germans returning fire from the gondolas. Sowrey then concentrated his third drum on one spot near the middle and was successful; the airship caught fire and descended to earth. It being a clear night, the chilling sight was seen from more than a hundred miles away by the crews of two other airships, L17 and L23, near Lincoln. All on board died in the inferno. The wreckage of L32, which lay at Snails Hall Farm, Great Burstead, near Billericay in Essex, drew huge crowds the following morning, the public using every available means of transport to get there. Sowrey received the Distinguished Service Order and the German airmen were buried with full military honours and mixed emotions.

L32, seen here in flight, was shot down in flames near Great Burstead, Essex, by Second Lieutenant Frederick Sowrey, RFC. All the crew perished, including the commander, Oberleutnant zur See *Peterson.* Imperial War Museum

Next it was Mathy's turn, killed during a raid on London and the Midlands with six other Navy airships on 1/2 October. Commanding L31 again, he had approached London from the north but had been forced back by heavy gunfire, and deposited his bombs over Cheshunt in Hertfordshire. He then uncharacteristically dallied, giving time for aeroplanes to catch him up, one of which was piloted by twenty-six-year-old Second Lieutenant Wulstan J Tempest, RFC, who, like Robinson and Sowrey, belonged to No. 39 Squadron. Flying a BE2c, he had been patrolling above Hainault Farm when he saw the cigar-shape of L31 caught in a 'pyramid' of searchlights fifteen miles away at 11.45 pm. There was fog on the ground, but the sky was clear and starlit. According to Tempest's own account:

I made after her at all speed at about 15,000 feet altitude, gradually overhauling her. At this period the AA fire was intense, and I, being about five miles behind the Zeppelin, had an extremely uncomfortable time. At this point misfortune overtook me, for my mechanical pressure pump went wrong and I had to use my hand-pump to keep up the pressure in my petrol tank. This exercise at so high an altitude was very exhausting, besides occupying an arm, thus giving me 'one hand less' to operate with when I commenced to fire. As I drew up with the Zeppelin, to my relief I found that I was free from AA fire, for the nearest shells were bursting quite three miles away. The Zeppelin was now nearly 15,000 feet high and mounting rapidly. I therefore decided to dive at her, for though I held a slight advantage in speed, she was climbing like a rocket and leaving me standing. I accordingly gave a tremendous pump at my petrol tank and dived straight at her, firing a burst straight into her as I came. I let her have another burst as I passed under her and then, banking my machine over, sat under her tail, and flying along underneath her, pumped lead into her for all I was worth. I could see tracer bullets flying from her in all directions, but I was too close under her for her to concentrate on me. As I was firing, I noticed her begin to go red inside like an enormous Chinese lantern and then a flame shot out of the front part of her and I realized she

Second Lieutenant Sowrey seated in the BE2c which condemned L32 to death. Imperial War Museum

L31, the airship that was Kapitänleutnant *Mathy's last command and which was shot down at Potters Bar, Hertfordshire on 1/2 October, 1916. Taken at Nordholz, the figure in the left foreground is Peter Strasser, the leader of the Naval Airship Division.* Royal Air Force Museum

was on fire. She then shot up about 200 feet, paused, and came roaring straight down on to me before I had time to get out of the way. I nose-dived for all I was worth, with the Zepp tearing after me, and expected every minute to be engulfed in flames. I put my machine into a spin and just managed to corkscrew out of the way as she shot past me, roaring like a furnace. I righted my machine and watched her hit the ground with a shower of sparks. I then proceeded to fire off dozens of green Very's lights in the exuberance of my feelings.

L31 came down in a field at Potters Bar, in Hertfordshire. Mathy jumped out at the last minute and was reportedly found alive when discovered by locals, but died minutes later. He was thirty-three. Tempest, dizzy and exhausted after his strenuous efforts in the cold and low oxygen, suffered a fractured skull crash-landing at North Weald Basset. He subsequently received the Distinguished Service Order.

The next day *The Times* journalist, Michael MacDonagh, journeyed from King's Cross to report on the scene at Potters Bar. Much of London came with him:

The train I caught was packed. My compartment had its twenty seats occupied and ten more passengers found standing room in it. The weather, too, was abominable. Rain fell persistently. We had to walk the two miles to the place where the Zeppelin fell, and over the miry roads and sodden fields hung a thick, clammy mist. It was a joyful crowd all the same – very expressive of the racier spirit of London... The framework of the Zeppelin lay in the field in two enormous heaps, separated from each other by about a hundred yards. Most of the forepart hung suspended from a tree... The crew numbered nineteen. One body was found in the field some distance from the wreckage. He must have jumped from the airship from a considerable height. So great was the force with which he struck the ground that I saw the imprint of his body clearly defined in the stubbly grass. There was a round hole for the head, then deep impressions of the trunk, with outstretched arms, and finally the widely separated legs.

***The impression left in the ground by one of the crew who jumped from the
falling Zeppelin.*** **Imperial War Museum**

MacDonagh went from this gruesome detail to another, insisting on being allowed
into the barn where the bodies of the Germans had been put:

> *Explaining to the sergeant that I particularly wanted to see the body of the
> Commander, I was allowed to go in. The sergeant removed the covering from one of the
> bodies which lay apart from the others. The only disfigurement was a slight distortion
> of the face. It was that of a young man, clean-shaven. He was heavily clad in a dark
> uniform and overcoat, with a thick muffler round his neck. I knew who he was...
> Heinrich Mathy, the most renowned of the German airship commanders, and the
> perished airship was his redoubtable L31. Yes, there he lay in death at my feet, the
> bugaboo of the Zeppelin raids, the first and most ruthless of these Pirates of the Air bent
> on our destruction. He had poured hundreds of bombs indiscriminately on the
> defenceless civilian population in the darkness of night – this destroyer of humble
> homes, this slayer of women and children! And now he had met the fate that was fitting!*

Mathy had boasted to the *New York World* that he could raze London, words which
were reported worldwide. Now that he had been humbled, Britons could raise a wry
smile. But while they cursed the memory of this 'baby killer', Germans mourned
him as one of their nation's most illustrious war heroes. Considered to be the best
and boldest of the airship commanders, his loss was a great blow to the closely-knit
members of the Naval Airship Division.

It was nearly two months before another raid was attempted. On 27/28 November

Mathy's conqueror: Second
Lieutenant Wulstan Tempest, RFC
Imperial War Museum

Kapitänleutnant *Mathy, the best*
of the Zeppelin commanders.
Imperial War Museum

ten Zeppelins went against the Midlands and the North of England. Most failed to reach their objectives and yet another two were brought down. L34, commanded by *Kapitänleutnant der Reserve* Max Dietrich, was caught in searchlights over Hartlepool close to midnight. At 10,000ft Second Lieutenant Ian V. Pyott of No. 36 Squadron, RFC, chased it in his BE2c for five miles to pour bullets into its port side and set it ablaze, the terrific heat scorching his face. The Zeppelin fell vertically for several long minutes and broke up in the sea a mile offshore, all hands lost. Further south, near Lowestoft, L21 under *Oberleutnant zur See* Kurt Frankenberg suffered a similar fate at the hands of Flight Lieutenant Egbert Cadbury and Flight Sub-Lieutenant Edward L. Pulling, both RNAS. L21 had eluded several attackers as it steered south from Yorkshire and eventually east into Norfolk in the course of nine hours over England. It was just leaving the coast at six in the morning when its luck ran out and it was attacked by Cadbury and Pulling in their BE2cs. The Zeppelin crashed in flames in the sea, with no survivors.

This flurry of successes against the raiders in the autumn of 1916 boosted British morale and the resources that had been poured into Home Defence seemed to be working: at the end of the year over 17,000 officers and other ranks were devoted to air defence, anti-aircraft batteries and searchlights, and 110 aeroplanes formed the Home Defence squadrons. There would not be any more serious attacks for several months while the Germans licked their wounds. The indefatigable Strasser would spend that time developing the newest Zeppelins, the black under-sided 'height climbers'. These preferred height to speed, sacrificing crew space and an engine, and reducing fuel and the number of bombs they carried to enable them to reach a ceiling of 20,000ft, out of the range of aeroplanes. The German Army, meanwhile, was about to try its hand at bombing Britain again. Not with airships this time, but aeroplanes.

CHAPTER 4

Popular Responses

Zepp time… lasts a fortnight in each month and is a very annoying time.
Colonel Edward B. Bartley

Throughout the war the government imposed censorship on the reporting of the German air raids. This was designed both to prevent the Germans finding out how effective and accurate their attacks were and to keep the public calm. Its policy in the latter instance was a failure. The authorities' reluctance to divulge details about

A letter from April 1916 opened by the censor and censor's note asking the writer to omit any reference to Zeppelin raids. Imperial War Museum

CENSOR.

3166

APL 6 16

Mrs. J. M. Andrews

3044

OPENED BY CENSOR

Postal Censorship.

The communication returned in this cover constitutes a breach of the Defence of the Realm Regulations. The writer is warned to be more careful in future.

N.B.—The communication will be allowed to proceed if the passage or passages referring to *Zepplin raids de* are omitted, and if it is re-posted to the addressee in the usual way.

W 14215—235   5,000   12/15   H W V (P 1934/4)
18855—29   10,000   3/16

raid locations and the suppression of the number of casualties only made matters worse by encouraging the spread of wild rumours. The official description of raids as 'visits' drew scorn and derision, and the attempt at secrecy alienated many citizens who felt they had a right to know what was happening and what was being done about it. Not that the government was able to stop the spread of news. People could visit damaged areas for themselves or hear about incidents by word of mouth from friends or family. Although the censors investigated letters and returned them with a warning if they referred to air raids, they could only examine so many; thus the majority of mail sent around the country or posted to those fighting abroad avoided their scrutiny. Regardless of the futility of its efforts, though, the government persisted with its official line that the raids were insignificant and the newspapers faithfully portrayed the British as a cheerful and plucky lot, calm and unworried by the German air menace. This was a false picture, disguising a wide range of responses. For some the advent of the Zeppelins was an irksome nuisance and meant nothing more than the inconvenience of extinguishing one's lights lest the special constables impose a fine. For some the raids exerted a grim fascination, even excitement. For others, despite the many failed or ineffectual raids and the relatively small number of casualties inflicted, they were a terrifying ordeal hardly to be faced.

Cartoon from **Punch**, *September 1915. The Press liked to depict the British public as spirited and indomitable in the face of air raids. But attitudes were not so straightforward, or so singular.* Punch Publications

GRIT.

THE MORNING AFTER THE ZEPPELIN RAID IN OUR VILLAGE.

One of the common responses to witnessing a raid was the impotence and anger felt by the onlooker. In the case of J. H. Stapley, writing from London on 5 October 1915 to a friend at the Front, the sight made him more resolved against the Germans than ever:

> We saw a Zepp the other night... and I need hardly tell you it was simply awful to see that vile thing over our heads and we helpless to do anything. To see the blasted bombs being dropped on helpless civilians and on peaceable houses made the blood go to fever heat and I felt absolutely MAD. Anyhow they did some damage to poor little children and some harmless civilians going home from their daily toil, and the GermHun devils call it WAR. They don't know what war means, Mack and they shew it immediately that they get up against the British bayonets, behind which are boys of the Bulldog breed, like yourself, for they immediately begin to cry and whine like whipped curs. Yet when they can injure innocent, unharmed people they make a big crow, and shout, and wag and wave flags, and proclaim it as a great victory and that they have struck terror into the English people in London. Well I can only say this, that it has had the effect of making the Londoners, at any rate, more determined than ever that the GermHun power shall not only be only beaten but ABSOLUTELY CRUSHED out of existence.

In other cases, perhaps less common but no less noteworthy, the raids presented a diverting spectacle, something like a 'show'. Miss K. Bannerman, an eighteen-year-old Voluntary Aid Detachment worker at a Red Cross hospital in Mayfair, for example, found the experience of a raid in September 1915 utterly thrilling:

> I have lived through an air raid and I feel life has been worth living. Fancy an air raid on London – an epoch-making event and I might have missed it... I flew out of bed as soon as I realized what was happening and went into the other room where I saw the small luminous patch on which the searchlights were playing which was the Zepp, though I couldn't actually make out its shape as some girls did.
> We then bundled into some clothes and went downstairs into a dear fatherly old major's room and he shoved our heads out of the window and we saw the luminous cloud and the shrapnel bursting a good deal short of it.
> After that we went down to the bathroom where there were a few more patients some nurses had collected. All this time our guns were firing like mad, the sirens were hooting, whistles blowing and now we heard the fire engines racing to the scene not to mention people in the street. When things quietened down the matron packed them all off to bed but I stayed up watching the reflection of the burning fires, not at all nervous... The next morning everyone was frightfully excited, comparing notes... I was far too excited to be nervous except for the first moment... This is the nearest I have ever reached to being under fire and very exhilarating it was too.

The next day friends of Miss Bannerman toured the City to see the wrecked houses and offices, and were amazed by such visual delights as the hole through which a bomb had dropped. Harriet Ingleby, the wife of the MP, Holcombe Ingleby, expressed similar exuberance about an earlier raid in August:

> It was a most thrilling and wonderful sight... I turned out of bed and looking up I saw just above us 2 Zepps. The searchlights were on them and they looked as if they

were amongst the stars. They were up very high and like cigar-shaped constellations. They kept getting away from the searchlights only to be found out and caught again... then the guns began and the whole place was full of smoke... it all made an infernal row and all the time I felt as in a dream – can this be London?

Usually the response to raids was more equivocal, however. Watching Zeppelins raid London on 8/9 September 1915 had very different effects on Mr W. A. Phillips and his household. As he wrote in a letter:

I saw probably the most fascinating sight of my life, a regular battle in the air, as near as possible straight above our house at Muswell Hill. The Zepp with 3 searchlights dead on her was as plain as daylight and one shell burst so close to her that she rocked and quivered very perceptibly and then turned nose straight or almost so up in the air... Just after this the lights were switched off [and] two more were seen. The noise of the guns and shells bursting and the bombs exploding was terrific and most awesome. It was a great sight but I hope to be spared seeing it again. Women simply went off their heads and were difficult to control. I locked my lot, wife and all, in the kitchen, but in less than ¹/₂ a minute they were out through the window.

More often than not, to experience a raid or an alarm was to *suffer* it. A letter from 'Harry and Blanche' in York, for example, reveals the absolute panic that was caused there when L21 raided the city on the night of 2 May 1916:

I have seen a bit in my time and I have a bit of nerve but I never want to see any

No one and nowhere was safe: First World War air raid precautions on the roof of Buckingham Palace, including steel braces, sandbags and wire netting. Imperial War Museum

*more of this. Women and children running about screaming and in their nightgowns...
it has unnerved everybody. People are today walking about with a vacant,* potty *stare
on their faces.*

In other instances people were unable to describe the event or even think about it
afterwards. Whole nights could be spent sleepless, sobbing and trembling, expecting
a bomb to burst overhead at any moment – and not only on nights when the alarm,
false or otherwise, had been raised. The fact that the capital of England was
vulnerable to attack, even though it enjoyed the best defences, was not reassuring.
As well as an attack on British pride, it meant that anyone, anywhere in Britain, was
at threat from the raiders. Bombs did not distinguish according to social rank, age,
sex, civilian or military status: no one and nowhere was safe.

The fact that innocent civilians were targets was an outrage, the death of children
a particularly wicked act of barbarity. Air raids constituted an 'unfair' type of warfare
and, it should be remembered, a new one. The diary of Mrs Ethel Bilbrough, from
Chislehurst in Kent, reveals just how novel the air raids felt in 1915 and 1916, and
how they brought home the war:

> *Things in the papers always seem so far away, it's only when one sees and hears* for
> oneself, *that the real horrors of war become apparent... the strain and anxiety of
> listening to unknown and terrifying sounds – sounds* never *heard before... What a*
> degrading *war this is besides being a bloodthirsty and terrible one. The poisonous
> gasses, the Zeppelins, the torpedoes, and the hidden treacherous mines, all strike a note
> of* mean unfairness; *in modern slang it's simply 'not cricket'... But as someone said
> the other day, 'There are no civilians now, we are all soldiers'.*

The dread caused by the threat of raids had more effect on people's daily lives and
war production than the actual bombs that were dropped. Alarms and false alarms
reduced the morale and effectiveness of the labour force, affecting nightshift workers
in particular, and making day workers late after a raid. Factories were sometimes
abandoned and transport ground to a halt. Fears in the capital were such that as
many as half a million citizens at a time sought shelter in the ninety or so
Underground stations and London's tunnels, such as at Blackwall, Greenwich and
Woolwich. They took with them as many household goods as they could carry,
squatting there in unsanitary conditions all evening and sometimes all night, raid or
no raid. In other cities some inhabitants headed for the countryside in favourable
weather to sleep under the open skies. If they could, people moved away from the
worst hit areas, sent their children away, or kept them home from school.

With all the aggravation the air raids caused, it is little wonder that retaliatory
measures were called for against Germany. It is also unsurprising that, when alarms
were genuine and fears became grievances, the majority of Britons bayed for the
blood of the 'baby killers'. What is interesting is that many preserved a sense of
humanity in their attitude to the men of the Zeppelins. There were individuals who
felt concerned and guilty at their own or others' glee when an aircrew was cremated
alive in their doomed airship. There were pilots such as Flight Lieutenant Cadbury,
who helped to shoot down L21 on 27/28 November 1916. He felt no satisfaction in
condemning the German crew to a horrific death off Great Yarmouth and refused to
join in the other pilots' celebrations when they returned to base.

CHAPTER 5

The Coming of the Gothas

There is no doubt in my mind that the effect of all warlike bombing and destructive devices, that is the one which is the most depressing on a man. I have talked to soldiers who time after time had experienced in the trenches heavy artillery fire, but they regarded it as quite enjoyable compared with lying helpless waiting for German bombers to drop their loads.
Major Tryggve Gran, RFC

Although there had been aeroplane attacks on Britain since early in the war, these were one off, opportunistic sorties mainly involving seaplanes. They were neither used in conjunction with the airships, nor were they sustained. But they did score a few 'firsts'. Thus, a Friedrichshafen FF29 floatplane of the German Seaplane Unit (*See Flieger Abteilung*) flying from occupied Belgium can claim to have carried out the first ever raid against Britain, on 21 December 1914, a month before the Zeppelins began their campaign in early 1915. The two small bombs it dropped fell in the sea off Dover's Admiralty pier, however, so the first bomb to land on Britain had to wait till three days later, on the 24th, when another Friedrichshafen FF29 followed the same route and dropped a single explosive device close to Dover Castle. There was little damage except for a few broken windows. These insignificant raids, then, were hardly the shape of things to come.

Hauptmann *Ernst Brandenburg, the leader of the 'England Squadron', sitting at his desk in Melle-Gontrode. He wears the* **Pour le Mérite,** *awarded him by the Kaiser in June 1917.* **Imperial War Museum**

A Gotha bomber in flight. Imperial War Museum

The German Army had envisaged an aeroplane squadron for the systematic bombing of Britain from the beginning of the war and had formed a unit at Ghistelles with this specific objective. To disguise their intentions the squadron was named the Ostend Carrier Pigeon Squadron (*Brieftauben Abteilung*) and the best pilots in service were transferred to it. However, it required a base as close to England as Calais before it could be of use, and when the German Army failed to take the Channel coast in the first months of the war the squadron's ineffective range from within Belgium meant the project was abandoned for the time being. The Army turned to airships because of their greater range and bomb capacity, but dissatisfaction and disasters with these soon made the Army concentrate its efforts on creating aeroplanes that were capable of longer distances and could carry more credible payloads. What they came up with was the Gotha bomber, 'Gotha' referring to their place of manufacture. The G IVs had a wingspan of 78ft and were 40ft long; powered by twin 260hp Mercedes engines, they were capable of 80mph and had a ceiling up to 15,000ft fully loaded. They were armed with three machine guns positioned one in the nose and two in the rear, one of the latter peeping out from beneath the fuselage to protect what usually for aeroplanes was a blind spot. To provide the extra security of covering fire Gothas would fly together in a tight formation – usually a rising V-shape with aircraft behind being slightly higher than those in front. The three-man crew consisted of a commander-navigator (and bomber), pilot and rear gunner. The bomb load generally consisted of four 50kg (110lb) bombs, ten 25kg (55lb) bombs and a number of incendiaries.

An observer-gunner in the nose of a Gotha, with an oxygen tube in his mouth. Imperial War Museum

The Gothas possessed certain advantages over their airship counterparts. They were far less visible and, being aeroplanes, if they were spotted they were less easily identifiable as enemy craft. The fact that they were intended for daylight raids, as opposed to the night-time attacks of the Zeppelins, facilitated navigation and allowed them to abandon wireless direction finding, which in turn meant that the British would have no signals to intercept warning of their coming. But a problem with the Gothas was the difficulty that their crews had in landing, due to the aircraft returning lighter after depositing their bombs and using up petrol. Crash landings were in fact to destroy more of these aeroplanes than anything else during their period of service, including hostile action.

A Gotha airman inflates his jacket before flying. Imperial War Museum

Led by *Hauptmann* Ernst Brandenburg, the Gothas were formed into Kagohl 3 (short for *Kampfgeschwader der Obersten Heeresleitung* 3 – Battle Squadron 3 of the Army High Command) which was later, at the end of 1917, renamed Bogohl 3 (short for *Bombengeschwader*), and otherwise known as the 'England Squadron', or *Englandgeschwader*. This was based at the St Denis-Westrem and Melle-Gontrode aerodromes close to Ghent in northern Belgium where by May 1917 four flights of six bombers each had been assembled. What intelligence Britain had received about the England Squadron was slow to be passed on and there was an assumption that the planes were intended for tactical missions on the Western Front, like their G III predecessors, rather than for strategic bombing in England. Thus the raid on 25 May 1917 came as a complete surprise.

At four in the afternoon that day twenty-three Gothas took off from their two bases. One suffered engine trouble and another crashed in the sea, but the remaining twenty-one crossed the Essex coast at 5.00 pm, unidentified by the complacent Home Defence. Due to hazy conditions over the capital, Brandenburg decided to turn the squadron south and aim for the important supply port of Folkestone on the Kent coast. They arrived there at 6.00 pm, after dropping several bombs on an airfield at nearby Lympne, and bombed the town and neighbouring Army camp at Shorncliffe. Those on the ground had no idea that they were German planes and no air raid warning had been given. The area near the docks was badly hit, especially Tontine Street with its crowded shops – there was carnage as a whole premises disappeared with its customers. After ten minutes of hell the Gothas flew home. RFC and RNAS aeroplanes pursued them, but the Gothas' formation largely held firm. One straggler was hit by Flight Sub-Lieutenant Reginald Leslie, RNAS, flying a Sopwith Pup, who saw smoke and steam pour from it. He could not confirm the kill, but he had the consolation of a Distinguished Service Cross for his valiant effort. Nine Pups of the RNAS squadrons at Dunkirk engaged the Gothas as they reached the Belgian coast at 18,000ft and claimed to have shot down one and seen another fall out of control. The Germans admitted the loss of only one. The England Squadron had killed ninety-five and injured 195 in the Kent raid, figures which included a number of soldiers – mostly Canadians – but of which the majority were women and children. Understandably, the British public was outraged. Censors tried to hide which town had been bombed, but secrecy merely spawned rumour: the number of casualties was increased tenfold and some even thought the Germans had invaded.

The Gothas returned on the afternoon of 5 June when twenty-two struck at the port and arsenal at Sheerness in Kent. They flew in via the North Sea and Essex as they had done the first time, though in this instance the defence forces were more alert. The strike was sudden and lasted less than five minutes, bombs raining on Shoeburyness and the Sheerness harbour. Fainting women were told it was only a practice, to try to keep them calm, but there was mayhem in the High Street which was crowded with women and children. One Gotha which ventured too low was brought down by AA and some of the German bombs failed to explode; still, the raid resulted in the deaths of thirteen, and thirty-four injured. The squadrons at Dunkirk challenged the bombers on their way back and inflicted damage on several, but none were destroyed.

A little over a week later, on 13 June, twenty-two Gothas set out on a clear day from their Belgian bases, seventeen of which approached London from the north-west. Anti-aircraft fire burst inadequately short of the raiders at 15,000ft, no doubt due to the fact that, because of their size, which was considerably greater than that of fighter aircraft, the Gothas appeared low seen from the ground. Watched by thousands of curious Londoners who were enjoying the warm sunshine and imagined the planes to be friendly, the Gothas sought their targets. The leader of the German bombers, *Hauptman* Brandenburg, wrote in his flight report:

> *Visibility was exceptionally good. With perfect clearness, the Thames bridges, the railway stations, the city, even the Bank of England, could be recognized. The anti-aircraft fire over London was not particularly strong and was badly directed... Our aircraft circled round and dropped their bombs with no hurry or trouble.*

Another of the German bombers related his excitement as he intently sighted with his telescope:

> *Slowly long rows of streets pass the small orbit of the sight. At last it is time to drop. I give a signal and in less time than it takes to tell, I have pushed the levers and anxiously follow the flight of the released bombs. With a tremendous crash they strike the heart of England. It is a magnificently terrific spectacle seen from midair. Projectiles from hostile batteries are sputtering and exploding beneath and all around us, while the earth below seems to be rocking.*

One other airman likened pressing the bomb release above London to delivering the greetings of the German people to the English. Greetings indeed. The Gothas first bombed the docks, then droned west and struck Liverpool Street Station, killing thirteen railway staff and passengers. A famous eyewitness to the tragedy was the war poet Siegfried Sassoon, an officer in the Royal Welch Fusiliers convalescing in Britain after being wounded in France, who was trying to make his way by train to Cambridge. He recalled the event and the profound impression it made upon him in his *Memoirs of an Infantry Officer:*

> *It was impossible to deny that the War was being brought home to me. At Liverpool Street there had occurred what, under normal conditions, would be described as an appalling catastrophe. Bombs had been dropped on the station and one of them had hit the front carriage of the noon express to Cambridge. Horrified travellers were hurrying away. The hands of the clock indicated 11.50; but railway time had been interrupted; for once in its career, the imperative clock was a passive spectator. While I stood wondering what to do, a luggage trolley was trundled past me; on it lay an elderly man, shabbily dressed, and apparently dead. The sight of blood caused me to feel quite queer. This sort of danger seemed to demand a quality of courage dissimilar to front line fortitude. In a trench one was acclimatized to the notion of being exterminated and there was a sense of organised retaliation. But here one was helpless; an invisible enemy sent destruction spinning down from a fine weather sky; poor old men bought a railway ticket and were trundled away again dead on a barrow; wounded women lay about in the station groaning.*

Within two minutes over seventy-two bombs had fallen in a mile radius of Liverpool Street Station, hitting offices and the Royal Mint. But the most shocking incident occurred further east, at Poplar in the docklands area, where a 50kg (110lb) bomb

An airraid notice printed in response to the bombing of Upper North Street School in Poplar, in which eighteen children were killed by a Gotha's bomb. Imperial War Museum

fell on the Upper North Street School. It penetrated three floors, killing two pupils in the process, and then exploded in the basement among a class of infants claiming the lives of a further sixteen and injuring many more. This contributed to a total of 162 dead, 432 injured that day, the highest toll of the war for a single air raid.

The German airmen returned home safely from their enterprise, unconcerned by AA or the squadrons of the Home Defence. Flying a Sopwith Pup, Captain James McCudden, RFC, one of the most distinguished and skilled British air aces of the First World War, was enraged at his inability to bring down the rearmost raider. He fired off three drums of bullets with his Lewis machine gun to no effect, commenting afterwards:

How insolent these damned Boches did look, absolutely lording the sky over England!... I was absolutely furious to think that the Huns should come over and bomb London and have it practically all their own way. I simply hated the Hun more than ever.

The nation fumed too, and grieved in equal measure, with many convinced that the Poplar school had been deliberately targeted. The opinion in Germany of the attack was different, of course, and a government telegram between Berlin and Amsterdam actually blamed Britain for the civilian casualties, because civilians had not been removed from war centres such as London and Dover. German moral self-assurance was such that the Kaiser presented Brandenburg with the *Pour le Mérite* for the raid. The Gotha leader was badly hurt in a flying accident returning from the presentation ceremony, though, and while he was out of action his command devolved to *Hauptmann* Rudolf Kleine.

The air raid initiative had clearly passed from airships to aeroplanes. The day after the massed aeroplane attack on England's capital one of the most up-to-date Zeppelins, L43, was brought down near the Dutch coast by a RNAS flying boat. Strasser, in a rash effort to impress and reassure the Kaiser, hastily ordered six 'height climbers' for a raid against England on the short summer night of 16/17 June. Only two were able to complete the North Sea crossing and two never even left

Hauptman *Rudolf Kleine, who stood in for Brandenburg as leader of the England Squadron after the latter was injured.* Imperial War Museum

their sheds because of strong winds. Although L42 managed to drop three bombs on Ramsgate and evade pursuit by soaring out of range of its attackers, L48, the very latest of the 'height climbers', was caught as it lingered at dawn over East Anglia with failing engines and compass. Although technically capable of a height of 20,000ft, its commander *Kapitänleutnant der Reserve* Franz Eichler had been forced to descend to 13-14,000ft to take advantage of tailwinds to return home. The vulnerable airship was set upon by three British aeroplanes and shot down in flames, falling at Holly Tree Farm, near Theberton in Suffolk. Remarkably, three of the crew survived the fall, although one succumbed afterwards to his injuries. Among the lucky survivors was a machinist, Heinrich Ellerkamm. When the Zeppelin caught fire and fell, he braced himself against a girder and supporting wires near the bow of the craft, which was falling slowly stern first. As he listened to the screams of his crewmates and his fur coat started to catch fire, death seemed inevitable. Thoughts rushed through his mind:

> What about jumping overboard and finishing the business? We had often discussed such a situation in Nordholz. There was only one thing to do, we decided: get out! jump for it! don't stop there to be burnt alive! But it's a bitter thing to do; one thinks a lot in moments like that – silly things perhaps, but they are all about the bright side of life. I was expecting a fortnight's leave, and Gretel, my fiancée, was waiting to see me. And was I to die here?

Luckily for him, he didn't jump, for the next instant the Zeppelin hit the ground and crashed into pieces beneath him, breaking his fall. Only slightly injured, he was able to crawl away from the burning wreckage and the burst oil and benzene tanks, to

Naval Zeppelin L48, brought down in flames near Theberton, 17 June 1917. Its commander was Kapitänleutnant der Reserve Franz Eichler, and on board with him was Korvettenkapitän Viktor Schütze. The blackened underside, to reduce visibility, was common to the 'height climbers' and later Zeppelins. Imperial War Museum

The Central Telegraph Office, London, set alight by Gotha incendiaries in a daylight raid on 7 July 1917. Falling rubble killed a sentry in the street below. Imperial War Museum

Firemen dampening smouldering ruins in Little Britain, following the Gotha raid on the capital, 7 July 1917. Imperial War Museum

become a prisoner of war. Among the dead, however, was *Korvettenkapitän* Schütze, who had assumed command of the Naval Airship Division on Strasser's appointment as overall Leader of Airships.

The destruction of L48 gave a boost to Home Defence, making up a little for the impudence of the Gothas. The only answer was to secure better aeroplanes, and these could only come from the Western Front. Reluctantly and under intense pressure, General Haig did allow two squadrons to be re-allocated for Home Defence, and then only for a strictly limited period. These squadrons had some of the best fighter-planes, SE5s and Sopwith Pups, but in the fortnight they were protecting England they achieved nothing, failing to counter an early morning hit-and-run raid against Harwich and Felixstowe on 4 July, during which eighteen Gothas led by Kleine easily repelled a DH4 flown by Captain J. Palethorpe, RFC, and killed his machine gunner, Air Mechanic J. O. Jessop. Two days after the extra squadrons returned to their duties in France Kagohl 3 renewed its efforts against London. On the morning of Saturday the 7th Kleine led twenty-one Gothas in formations along the north and south banks of the Thames. They arrived past the AA barrage in central London sometime after 10.00 am and inflicted fifty-four casualties. Dozens of British airmen engaged them above London and three were lost attacking the formations, but one Gotha that broke rank suffered the consequences and was brought down in the Thames estuary by Second Lieutenant Frederick A. D. Grace, RFC, and his observer, Second Lieutenant George Murray, in an Armstrong Whitworth FK8. Grace fired his Vickers gun as he closed on the enemy, then Murray took over with his Lewis gun, aiming at the mid-section of the Gotha till black smoke issued forth. The German aeroplane plummeted into the sea where its crew members drowned. Four German aeroplanes arriving back at base crash-landed, with the loss of one life.

The British Service chiefs who had authorized the return of the Western Front squadrons without the blessing of the government were embarrassed and Haig was again forced to relinquish one under protest. London's defences were reorganized as the London Air Defence Area (LADA), commanded by Brigadier General E. B. Ashmore (afterwards Major General).

The next opportunity for Kleine to strike came on Sunday, 22 July. In London for the first time, maroons – sound bombs used as distress signals at sea – were fired to alert the public. Hitherto, the government had been unwilling to issue general alarms, fearing they would cause too much disruption; now, though, public safety was paramount. But the capital was not the Gothas' intention. Instead, they aimed at the ports supplying the build-up to Haig's planned offensive at Ypres, Harwich and Felixstowe. These were bombed at 8.00 am by twenty-one aeroplanes, killing thirteen and injuring twenty-six. The Gothas wreaked little material damage, however, and the effect on Haig's preparations was negligible. Such tactical bombing was small change compared with the strategic and morale value of a raid on London and the German Army Command should really have known better. On 12 August twelve Gothas attempted to raid Chatham naval base, but were deflected by anti-aircraft fire and turned their attention to Southend. Within a quarter of an hour they killed thirty-two and wounded forty-six. Returning home, one straggling German aeroplane was intercepted by Flight Sub-Lieutenant H. S. Kerby, RNAS, a veteran of the Western Front. He shot it down in the sea, for which he received the

Distinguished Service Cross, but it offered little solace. The public was indignant that this holiday town had been bombed on a Sunday and the authorities were heavily criticized for failing to raise the alarm, despite having been warned that the raid was imminent. There was anger too that the AA batteries at nearby Sheerness and Eastchurch had not opened fire on the raiders; it seemed that they had adhered to the day of rest.

There were major setbacks for the England Squadron to come, however. Twenty-eight Gothas that set off in adverse weather on 18 August had to turn back after being blown off course. Two crews came down and were interned in Holland; two other crews were lost in the sea with all hands. Another raid was launched on 22 August, fifteen planes setting out for Dover, Margate and Ramsgate. But, after five turned back, the remainder lost formation as a result of determined anti-aircraft fire, allowing two intruders to be picked off by the Home Defence squadrons and AA. To avoid further heavy casualties the German Army therefore took the decision to switch Kagohl 3's role to night bombing. The tactic worked: in the dark hours of 3/4 September four Gothas reconnoitred Chatham, during which hits were made against the naval establishment there. Two of their bombs landed in the centre of the depot, right on top of a drill hall that was being used as a dormitory where some thousand sailors were sleeping. Ordinary Seaman Frederick W. Turpin was in another building only 150 yards away when the explosion awakened him. He turned out with others and went to the scene to help with the wounded. He recorded what happened in his notebook:

A Gotha G V being loaded with 100kg (220lb) and 50kg (110lb) bombs.
Imperial War Museum

It was a gruesome task. Everywhere we found bodies in a terribly mutilated condition. Some with arms and legs missing and some headless. The gathering up of the dismembered limbs turned one sick... It was a terrible affair and the old sailors, who had been in several battles, said they would rather be in ten Jutlands or Heligolands than go through another raid such as this.

One hundred and thirty-two were killed and almost a hundred were wounded in the incident; the bombs responsible were the two deadliest to fall on Britain in the whole of the war. There had been no alarm and the defensive batteries, searchlights and aeroplanes were completely evaded. It seemed night-time defence had been forgotten.

The next night a larger reconnaissance was made, this time employing nine aeroplanes over London (a tenth was shot down by AA at Sheerness). In the half-hour before midnight the Strand and Victoria Embankment were badly hit, killing nineteen and injuring seventy-one. In response, London's defences were tweaked once more. The guns were moved further away from the centre of London to try and

A balloon apron used in the defence of London. Imperial War Museum

fence it off and sound-location posts were established to track the Gothas' movements. To replace the batteries in inner London, on 5 September Ashmore instigated lines of barrage balloons. These comprised three balloons at a time carrying a cable 2,000 yards long, from which hung a series of wires 1,000ft in length. These 'aprons' acted both as a physical barrier and, by instructing pilots not to fly at less than 10,000ft within the barrage line, a means of concentrating anti-aircraft fire without threatening friendly aeroplanes. In late 1917 18-pounder British guns would replace the established French 75mm AA. These were less accurate and had less range than their continental counterparts, but they were more serviceable for barrage fire, that is, where different guns combined their fire to create a line or wall of exploding shells – far more effective at night than each gun trying to pinpoint an often unseen raider. Furthermore, the British shrapnel fragmented better than the French shells, thus reducing the danger to civilians below.

While London prepared itself, the German Army High Command instigated a succession of night attacks between 24 September and 1/2 October, in what became known as the 'harvest moon' raids. The intensive air bombardment exhausted Home Defence personnel and frayed London's nerves. Lilah Morrison-Bell, the wife of the MP, Sir Clive, wrote to her husband detailing the situation she found in the capital when she and their young daughter, Shelagh, returned on a train from Edinburgh, arriving in King's Cross just as one of the air raids began:

At 7.30 I heard the first guns begin, and then the sky was all lit up by shrapnel bursting and the noise was terrific. It was no longer a case of trying to conceal matters from Shelagh or divert her attention, but I told her they were fireworks and called her attention to the lights, and luckily she believed me and wasn't a bit frightened. I must say one felt a bit unprotected in a train while this inferno was going on. On arrival at King's Cross there wasn't a porter to be seen, and everyone tore out of the train and rushed wildly for shelter... The station was a sight to see – crowds and crowds of poor people from the slums all round King's Cross had assembled and brought their beds and furniture and babies, and had encamped there under this concrete archway, and a policeman told me they come every night and stay all night!... One could hear the dull thud of bombs falling, so different from the roar of the guns. They truly do make a desperate noise. Every few minutes there was silence, which was more nervy than the roar of the bombardment, and then the guns would begin again as the raiders tried to attack from a new position. In one of these silences a poor woman in the crowd flung her arms round my shoulders and buried her face in my coat, and another woman near me gave a wild shriek and fainted, and it was rather horrible hearing her fall heavily in that dense crowd. And when she came to, the guns were just at their loudest and she must have wished she had stayed unconscious I expect!

The hearty Mrs Morrison-Bell actually started to enjoy the spectacle and climbed up on a pile of luggage for a better view of the enemy aeroplanes, which were brilliantly lit against the moon. But clearly she was in a minority. A Scottish officer who had been quartered in Edinburgh for two years and had never experienced a raid before was so nervous that he turned white, and Mrs Morrison-Bell had to comfort him. The effect of the bombing was clearly demoralizing, but when she commented on this it provoked a reassuringly brave reply:

Damage in King's Cross Road, caused during the first of the 'harvest moon'
raids on the capital, 24 September 1917. Imperial War Museum

> *Once when I sat talking to the officer during the raid... I said to him, 'Well, the Germans will get what they want if they go on coming every night like this – they'll terrorize London into begging for peace terms' – and a poor man in the crowd who overheard my remark shouted out, 'No, you're quite wrong – English people will never do that, don't you worry. You don't know what the British people are like if you think that.'*

Sixty-nine were killed and 260 injured in that week, figures lower than might have been expected for such a sustained offensive, especially as the Gothas had been supplemented by the deadly new Giants, monsters that Britain was soon to see more of.

Although government officials expressed satisfaction with the level of casualties compared with the other theatres of the war, the British public found hard to accept the seeming impunity with which the Germans struck at the island. The damaging effect on morale at home spread to the troops abroad through correspondence. The series of depressing and alarming letters written by Edna Bentley to her husband in the artillery about air raids on Walthamstow, London, serve as an example:

> *Well darling such a sight I've never seen and hope not to again, talk about a swarm of birds wasn't in it. They were all over us in less than 10 mins and no warning was given whatever, and I never thought Rosie [their daughter] and I would be alive now. I wished you goodbye dearest with dear little Rosie clenched in my arms.*

She finished the letter in haste as another raid began. Other missives describe in grim detail places familiar to her husband that had been bombed – the grocers, the local pub and so on – and how she had prepared herself to meet the Supreme Father. She meant it when she wrote, 'Oh darling this life is getting too terrible for words and one's nerves cannot stand much more'.

Concerned husbands, fiancés and boyfriends could offer little comfort in reply. Some responded with advice about what to do in the event of a raid, usually urging their loved ones out of doors at the first hint of an alarm and to lie down flat; the greatest fear was that by taking refuge in a cellar or sheltering indoors one risked being buried alive. Others wrote back from Flanders expressing their own anxiety, such as Private John Mudd to his wife Lizzie: 'You know dear it's hard to be out here fighting and yet your wife and children can't be safe'. Many in the trenches said they preferred to take their chances there than experience an air raid. They grew increasingly angry about the attacks back home and sometimes this boiled over. When a German aeroplane was brought down in France in September 1917 the pilot was identified with the air raids simply by virtue of being an airman, even though he had no personal connection with the attacks on Britain. He was surrounded by a hostile crowd of infantrymen who began pelting him with sods of earth; they were only restrained from further, more fatal, violence by the intervention of officers who threatened them with their pistols.

The coming of the Gothas had intensified the demand for reprisals against Germany, both for reasons of revenge and as a means of deterring the air raids. Following the harrowing events at the Poplar school in June 1917, for instance, Royal Army Medical Corp (RAMC) Orderly Joe Evans wrote to his mother:

> *It is very sad to think of these poor kiddies and their mothers. If ever a crime called to heaven for vengeance, that one does. I hope they will speedily be repaid with interest.*

Adding later:

> *There is only one effective means of defence and I hope the government will be forced to make it* – reprisals.

These views were representative, but they were also largely ignored. Unlike in the Second World War, there was little or no counter-bombing of German cities; the strategic initiative lay almost all the time with the enemy. The British generals were too occupied with the lines in France and Belgium to take the air defence of Britain seriously, let alone consider bombing Germany. If they had been more willing to accept the serious effects that the German raids had on Britain they might have realized the sense in retaliation, but their concerns were overwhelmingly tactical. They were unwilling rather than unable to respond in like manner and it would not be until near the end of the war in 1918 that limited strategic bombing of Germany was undertaken. As Joe Evans scathingly commented:

> *A pity some of those responsible for the air defence, or non-defence, don't have a bomb or two dropped behind them. Perhaps they would get a move on if that happened.*

CHAPTER 6

Giants in the Sky

Those tiny school babes, our little ones,
Had ceased their task and were listening with bated breath,
For the blotting out of the glorious sun
By the broken thunder of the German Death.
Verse commemorating children killed in German air raids.

'Giant' is the common name for the Staaken R IV, R V and R VI aeroplanes, Staaken being the town near Berlin where they were built. The 'R' stood for *Riesen*-type, as in Giant-type, and their squadron was known as the *Riesenflugzeugen* or Giant Squadron. The name is appropriate. With a wingspan greater than 138ft, they were more than double the size of their Gotha counterparts. The R IV type had six engines powering two pushers and one tractor propeller, the R V had five engines powering three tractor propellers, and the R VI had four 260hp Mercedes or 245hp Maybach engines which drove two of each type of propeller. They had a speed up to 80mph and were capable of bearing two tons of bombs more than 300 miles. Usually they were armed with three machine guns, but they could carry up to six. Crew numbered between seven and nine, and consisted of the commander – who also performed the roles of navigator and bomber – two pilots, two flight mechanics, a fuel mechanic and a wireless operator. State-of-the-art cockpit features on board the Giants included a position-finding wireless transmitter. The R-plane Squadron, Rfa 501, was based at

*'Giant' bomber R39, which was commanded by **Hauptmann Richard von Bentivegni**, leader of the **Riesenflugzeugen**. Giant engine nacelles were large enough each to contain a cockpit for a flight mechanic, for him to be on hand for repairing any faults in mid-flight. In this photograph the engines are being tested and a flight mechanic seated in the port engine is just visible. **Imperial War Museum***

St Denis-Westrem and Melle-Gontrode in 1917, along with the Gothas, but from March 1918 they occupied a specially built aerodrome at Scheldewindeke, also close to Ghent. They were commanded by *Hauptmann* Richard von Bentivegni.

The Giants' advent in September 1917 did not mean the end of airship and Gotha attempts against Britain, and for several months Zeppelins and Gothas attacked without them. On the night of 19/20 October, in what was afterwards known as the 'Silent Raid', eleven German Navy 'height climbers' set out from their bases for industrial targets in northern England. Unfortunately for them, they encountered severe northerly gale-force winds at high altitude that blew them disastrously off course. All became lost and only L45, commanded by *Kapitänleutnant* Waldemar Kölle, was able to recognize London when it unintentionally passed over the city. A helmsman on the Zeppelin later recalled the captain and crew's surprise at this unforeseen opportunity:

At about 11.30 we began to see lights below, and as the lights continued, so it suddenly dawned on us that it could only be the city of London that we were flying over. Even Kölle looked amazed at the dim lights as Schutz suddenly shouted, 'London!' It was then that we realized the fury of the savage tempest that had been driving us off

Albany Road in Camberwell, London, after the 'Silent Raid' of 19/20 October 1917. Ten were killed and over twenty injured here when a 300kg (660lb) bomb demolished three houses. The explosive was dropped by Zeppelin L45, under the command of Kapitänleutnant Waldemar Kölle. Imperial War Museum

our course. But Kölle clearly had just one thought – that was higher. So he released more ballast and the bombs – first two sighting shots and then the rest. Over London! We had achieved what no other German airship had done since Mathy had bombed that proud city over a year ago! And his last trip across the City had been his undoing. Fortunately for us, we were unseen; not a searchlight was unmasked; not a shot was fired; not an aeroplane was seen. If the gale had driven us off our course, it had also defeated the flying defences of the city! It was misty or so it seemed, for we were above a thin veil of cloud. The Thames we just dimly saw from the outline of the lights; I thought I saw two great railway stations, but the speed of the ship running before the gale was such that we could not distinguish much. We were half-frozen too, and the excitement was great. It was all over in a flash. The last big bomb was gone and we were once more over the darkness and rushing onwards.

The series of bombs that L45 managed to drop as it sped over the metropolis caused considerable damage. One of the devices, weighing 300kg (660lb), fell next to

A card in memory of some of those killed during the 'Silent Raid', eight of whom aged 5-18 were members of the same family. Imperial War Museum

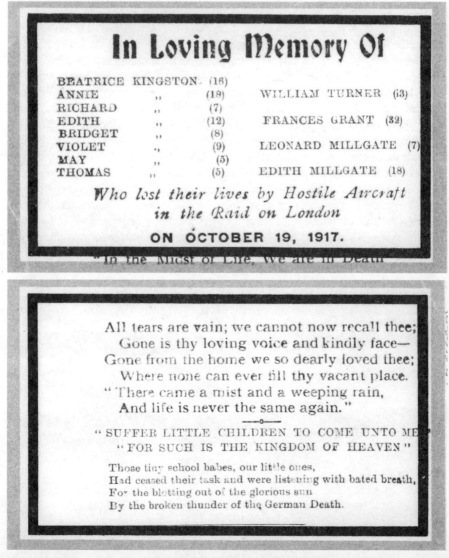

In Loving Memory Of

BEATRICE KINGSTON (16)
ANNIE   ,,   (18)   WILLIAM TURNER (13)
RICHARD   ,,   (7)
EDITH   ,,   (12)   FRANCES GRANT (32)
BRIDGET   ,,   (8)
VIOLET   ,,   (9)   LEONARD MILLGATE (7)
MAY   ,,   (5)
THOMAS   ,,   (5)   EDITH MILLGATE (18)

*Who lost their lives by Hostile Aircraft
in the Raid on London*

ON OCTOBER 19, 1917.

"In the Midst of Life, We are in Death"

All tears are vain; we cannot now recall thee;
  Gone is thy loving voice and kindly face—
Gone from the home we so dearly loved thee;
  Where none can ever fill thy vacant place.
"There came a mist and a weeping rain,
  And life is never the same again."

——o——

"SUFFER LITTLE CHILDREN TO COME UNTO ME"
"FOR SUCH IS THE KINGDOM OF HEAVEN"

Those tiny school babes, our little ones,
Had ceased their task and were listening with bated breath,
For the blotting out of the glorious sun
By the broken thunder of the German Death.

Piccadilly Circus where it killed seven and wounded sixteen. Dozens more were killed and hurt in Camberwell and Lewisham in south-east London. The Zeppelin's helmsman was right in saying that no attempt was made to bring the airship down. But the reason why London's guns were muted and the searchlights were switched off was in a vain attempt not to betray the capital to passing raiders such as L45. Lieutenant Commander Rawlinson afterwards recognized that the same storm-driven speed which would have protected the airship from AA also prevented it causing more damage than it had; he wisely commented that an 'act of God' had kept London from further harm rather than its defences. After trying for neutral Switzerland, L45 later came down near Sisteron in France where its crew fired the airship and surrendered. L49 landed in France at Bourbonne-les-Bains, AA at St Clement shot down L44 and L50 vanished without trace over the Mediterranean.

On 31 October it was the turn of the Gothas, when Kleine led twenty-two in a sortie against London with brand new 5kg (11lb) firebombs – the first time the England Squadron had attacked with incendiaries. There was intensive bombing of south-east London, but the raiders were deterred from approaching closer to the centre by the AA barrage. Fortunately for London's citizens, the supposedly improved incendiaries failed to cause the conflagration expected, many simply failing to go off, and, as a bonus, five of the German aeroplanes crash-landed on their return home. Giants finally reconvened with the Gothas on the frosty night of 5/6 December, when three Giants and sixteen Gothas attempted to carry out a three-part raid on Sheerness, Margate and Dover, and London. 420 bombs, most of them incendiaries, fell during the several hours of bombing, but they caused relatively few casualties – eight were killed and twenty-eight hurt. Once again, many of the firebombs failed to ignite, while the raiders bound for London, perturbed by closely bursting shells, discarded their payloads as quickly as they could and retired home. It seems that AA guns shot down three Gothas that night, one of the German aeroplanes crash landing at Rochford in Essex and another putting down near Canterbury, in Kent. Such losses took their toll on the England Squadron – hastily trained replacements meant that an increasing number of Gothas crashed on landing, and this of course led to less and less machines being available. To make matters worse, Kleine, who had been awarded the *Pour le Mérite*, was killed by a

A Staaken R VI bomber. Imperial War Museum

Canadian pilot, Captain Wendel Rogers, RFC, during a daylight attack near Ypres on 12 December.

Oberleutnant Richard Walter took charge of the demoralized squadron and showed himself a more cautious commander than Kleine. But this did not alter the downturn in Bogohl 3's misfortunes. An unsuccessful raid was launched on 18 December when the squadron attacked Canterbury, Margate and, along with a Giant, London. One of the Gothas, piloted by *Leutnant* Friedrich Ketelsen, became the first one to be brought down by a night fighter over Britain. Captain Gilbert Ware Murlis Green, No. 44 Squadron, RFC, spotted his exhaust flames at 7.15 in the evening, 10,000ft above Bermondsey. Murlis Green was careful to avoid the bombs dropped by the German and, despite being blinded by his own gun flash and the glare of a searchlight, his Camel inflicted enough damage on the Gotha to critically weaken its starboard engine. Although the aeroplane struggled away from the English pilot and reached the coast, it was unable to maintain height and decided to return to England, ditching in the sea off Folkestone. The trawler *Highlander* picked up two of the crew, but Ketelsen drowned. Murlis Green received a second Bar to his Military Cross.

The Germans had more luck in the New Year, when on 28/29 January 1918 one Giant and several Gothas infiltrated the capital's defences causing heavy casualties. The worst of this was achieved by the Giant, R12, which negotiated the anti-aircraft defences and fought off of a Bristol Fighter flown by Lieutenant John Goodyear, with First Class Air Mechanic Walter Merchant as his gunner. Goodyear had manoeuvred below the German aeroplane to give Merchant an opportunity to strafe it, but the Giant's machine guns got them first, rupturing the petrol tank and wounding Merchant. The Bristol Fighter was forced to land while R12 carried on and dropped a 300kg (660lb) bomb on Covent Garden soon after midnight. The explosive fell outside Odhams Printing Works in Long Acre, where 500 people were sheltering in the basement, a public air raid shelter. The blast caused the building to partially collapse, blocking two of the three exits, and fire engulfed the rest of the structure. Chaos ensued as those who could scrambled out, while those trapped inside were nearly drowned when water from firemen's hoses flooded the basement. Thirty-eight perished and eighty-five were hurt in this incident, making it the single most lethal bomb to have fallen on London. Five of the dead were employees of Messrs Odhams who heroically gave their lives rescuing others. Among the harrowing tales of the survivors, one might single out that of Mrs McGluskey, who not only lost a leg and fingers in the explosion but, worse, the baby she was cradling was blown out of her arms and disappeared forever.

Particularly unfortunate tragedies unfolded elsewhere in the city that night, when panic seized those seeking shelter at Bishopsgate railway goods depot in Shoreditch. Fourteen people, mostly women and children, were trampled to death there, contributing to the night's total of sixty-seven dead and 166 injured. The only consolation for Home Defence during the raid was the shooting down of one of the Gothas, commanded by *Leutnant* Friedrich von Thomsen. Two RFC Camels flown by Second Lieutenant Charles Banks and Captain George Hackwill sighted it over Romford, east London. They attacked and brought it down at Wickford in Essex with the loss of all three crew. Because they were the first pilots to bring down a Gotha on British soil, Banks and Hackwill were each awarded the Military Cross.

Odhams Printing Works in Long Acre, London. The basement was being used as a public air raid shelter when Giant R12 dropped a 300kg (660lb) bomb outside the building on 29 January 1918. Fire and falling masonry claimed thirty-eight lives and injured eighty-five. Imperial War Museum

The next night, 29/30 January, Britain endured the first raid to be conducted by Giants alone. While the England Squadron replaced its losses and concentrated on targets in France – on 31 January thirty-one Gothas bombed Paris, killing and wounding 259 – three Giants killed ten and injured ten in moonlit London. What is remarkable is that none of the bombers was brought down. In the course of the raid the largest of the Giants, R39, survived the attentions of Captain Arthur Dennis, RFC, who riddled its fuselage flying a BE12b, Second Lieutenant Bob Hall, RFC, who pursued it over Roehampton in a Camel, Captain F. L. Luxmoore, RFC, who took pot shots at it in another Camel, Captain George Hackwill, who fired 600 rounds at it to no avail from a third Camel, and, finally, a FK8 flown by Second Lieutenants Frank Bryant and V. H. Newton, RFC, as it reached the Channel on its way back. One of the other Giants, R25, also endured a series of attacks by five or more English planes. Despite losing a port engine to bullet damage, the Giant droned on towards London on its remaining three engines and discarded its bombs in fields after it lost too much height to climb over the Woodford–Southgate balloon apron. R25 then struggled home, unmolested by the twenty or so aircraft patrolling for it.

The Giant Squadron displayed further grit when they returned for another sortie on the Saturday night of 16 February. R12, commanded by *Oberleutnant* Hans-Joachim von Seydlitz-Gerstenberg, actually flew by mistake into the Woolwich balloon apron. The starboard wing clipped a cable and the aeroplane lurched out of control for 1,000ft before first pilot *Leutnant* Götte was able to restore order and direction. With admirable determination, the Giant continued on its mission and bombed Beckenham in the early hours of the morning. It returned home with only minor damage to the wing. Elsewhere, R39, commanded by *Hauptmann* von Bentivegni, dropped the first 1,000kg (2,200lb) bomb on England, the largest type to be used in the air raids. Von Bentivegni's bomb struck the Royal Hospital, Chelsea, demolishing the North Eastern Wing and killing a family of five, including two children. He was possibly aiming for Victoria Station half a mile away, but he did not get a second chance: because of the size of the bomb, it was the only one carried by the Giant.

The following night R25 attacked London on a solo mission. It was the only Giant serviceable from the evening before and was commanded by *Leutnant* Max Borchers. It appeared over Eltham in south-east London at around 10.00 pm, and began dropping 50kg (110lb) bombs in a north-westerly line across the city. Its final stack of six high explosives was released on St Pancras railway station and its Midland Grand Hotel. The blast wrecked the booking hall and first-class waiting room, and severely damaged the hotel ground floor: twenty-one people were killed, and a further twenty-two were injured, most of them while huddled beneath the hotel arch, watching the raid. The single Giant, which had succeeded in arousing everything Home Defence could muster, returned to base only slightly grazed by anti-aircraft fire.

When five Giants raided on 7/8 March they inflicted twenty-three fatalities and thirty-nine injuries, most of them in Maida Vale, west London, where another 1,000kg bomb was deposited by von Bentivegni aboard R39. It landed on and obliterated apartment buildings at numbers 61-67 Warrington Crescent, demolishing twenty surrounding houses and damaging another 120 along with it. The distressing scene that ensued is vividly described in a letter Mrs Bilbrough, of Chislehurst, received from her brother living in Randolph Crescent, which backed on to Warrington Crescent:

> *We got the 'warning' at 11.20, and went down into the basement; the guns had only just started when there was the most appalling awful crash that it is possible to describe... After the 'all clear' had gone I recollect forcing back the billiard room door (smashed off its hinges and filled with debris) and then we saw that awful sight of the houses across the garden all on fire, and reduced to ruins, many poor imprisoned people being below and powerless to get out, and I shall never forget their heartrending screams to my dying day. All night long hundreds of rescuers were working furiously, but it was over 15 hours before many bodies could be recovered.*

After this raid the Giants relented their attacks on Britain. They and the Gothas were largely devoted to tactical objectives behind the allied line in France as part of Germany's 1918 Spring Offensive, its last great push of the war – a final attempt to break the Anglo-French line and win the war before American troops arrived in sufficient numbers to condemn the Germans to defeat. Strategically, this was a mistake for Germany because the effect of the air raids on Britain – interrupting war production and diverting manpower and material – was more profound than what could be achieved on the Western Front. Although the temporary change offered a respite to the weary airmen, who found French targets less hazardous than British ones, a disaster befell Rfa 501 in May, a result not of hostile action but of negligence. Returning from a mission on the 9th, four Giants insisted on landing at their fog-engulfed base at Scheldewindeke, despite the availability of clearer landing strips close by. Although R39 made a safe landing, R29 was irreparably damaged and R32 and R26 were destroyed, losing nearly all on board. Among the remaining crews there was resentment at the glory-seeking von Bentivegni for risking his men and machines in poor weather.

Ten days after this the newly recovered Brandenburg organized what was to be the largest aeroplane raid on Britain, and, although he did not yet know it, also the last aeroplane raid. He mustered a strike force of thirty-eight Gothas and secured the support of three Giants, along with reconnaissance aeroplanes. On the night of Whitsunday, 19 May, while Gothas of Bogohl 6 conducted raids against military targets in northern France, killing 214 and injuring 700, the England Squadron and its allies set off for London. As many as ten Gothas were forced to turn back early for mechanical and other reasons, but eighteen, along with one Giant, breached the defences of the capital, while other members of the sortie targeted Southend, Rochester, Ramsgate and Dover. This massed German attack faced the most formidable British defence yet, the Home Defence squadrons bolstered by increasing numbers of Bristol Fighters, Camels and SE5as, and the German losses were consequently high. Two or more Gothas were brought down in flames off the coast by British batteries and four were shot out of the sky by aeroplanes.

One of the latter fell victim to nineteen-year-old Lieutenant Anthony J. Arkell and his gunner-observer, First Air Mechanic Albert Stagg, flying in Arkell's Bristol Fighter which he had christened 'Devil in the Dusk'. As part of No. 39 Squadron (now RAF), the two had taken off from their base at North Weald, Essex, when just after midnight they spotted something suspicious below them at 10,000ft, north of Hainault, and went to investigate. Arkell excitedly recounted the following mêlée in a letter to his father, the Reverend Arkell, written the same day:

> I dived down under it, as it was hazy, and then saw against the starlight the shape of a Gotha. What I thought were lights were the exhausts of the engines. I could see the 2 engines, and the long planes quite clearly. I soon caught it up. I was much faster and could climb better than it. After a little manoeuvring I got under its tail, about 150 yards behind. The observer Stagg fired 20 rounds, very scattered, and then stopped. I zoomed up level with its tail firing my front guns. Directly we started firing, it fired back. And when we weren't firing I could hear pop-pop-pop quite plainly. Stagg fired another drum of about 100 rounds; but, as his shooting wasn't very good, I decided the sooner we finished the Hun off the better, so got as close as I could underneath him. He was 3 times as big as we were. We were firing at point blank range, Stagg and I firing in turn. In the end Stagg fired the actual shot that set his right-hand petrol tank alight.

Arkell and Stagg between them had fired around 700 rounds by this time, with little

The remains of the Gotha destroyed by Lieutenant Anthony Arkell and First Air Mechanic Albert Stagg drew especially large crowds as 20 May was Whit Monday, a Bank Holiday. Imperial War Museum

damage in reply from the German. The Gotha had been gradually forced lower and lower during the scrap, and now it rolled over and crashed to the ground in a sheet of flame. *The Times* reported that the burning aeroplane was seen for miles around and 'Sirens, near and far, sounded a shrill note of victory, and from the watching people came a long and satisfied roll of cheering'. It came down in a bean field off Roman Road, 200 yards from Albert Dock, East Ham, by the north bank of the river Thames. Of the crew, two leapt to their deaths as the Gotha fell, the third was killed in the crash. The next morning Arkell visited the wreckage, which was less burnt up than he expected – only the rear and part of the fuselage had caught fire, the rest was just crashed, with the engines buried in the earth. Arkell collected a piece of the aeroplane's dark blue camouflage canvas, some charred wood, a cartridge case and a plywood ammunition box as souvenirs, and afterwards secured one of the propellers. Understandably, the young pilot was delighted with his feat, for which he received the Military Cross, and Stagg the Military Medal. But Arkell also had a sense of compassion, admitting of the enemy crew:

> I couldn't help feeling sorry for the poor fellows. For after all they were only acting under orders, and it must take very brave men to come all that way at night over the sea and hostile country.

British casualties for the night of the last aeroplane raid were forty-nine dead and 177 injured. The German official statement for the night's raid was reassuring and self-satisfied about the result: 'London, Dover, and other places on the English coast were successfully attacked with bombs'. But the German Army could not sustain its losses. Henceforth, its bombers would be used solely in mainland Europe rather than risk lives and aeroplanes above Britain.

In the summer of 1917 German airmen were full of confidence, setting off from Belgium in the late evening, laden with bombs; they would find the Thames and follow it to London unperturbed by British AA and aeroplanes, select their targets carefully and exult in the fire and smoke they caused beneath them, before turning and bidding Britain *auf wiedersehen*. By the spring of 1918, however, the violent reception awaiting them from the improved AA batteries rocked their nerves and the increased number of searchlight beams blinded their eyes; they were forced to fly high to avoid the balloon barrage, which left them feeling giddy and unable to make out much of the capital below. Rather than linger, they dropped their bombs indiscriminately and made a dash for the Channel, desperately hoping to avoid the attention of the now swarming British fighters. Abandoning the air raids on Britain therefore came as a welcome relief.

This was less true for members of the Giant squadron than it was for the Gotha crews, however. In all their raids on Britain not one Giant had been shot down. Partly this was luck, but it was mainly due to the remarkable resilience and size of the leviathans, which posed considerable problems for Home Defence. From the ground, observers often mistook single Giants for groups of seven or more Gothas; experimental listening posts experienced similar confusion, interpreting the drone of a Giant for a whole squadron of lesser planes. As such, one alone would lure into the sky all the British squadrons from miles about and panic the AA into firing at phantoms. When British pilots managed to track down a Giant, they usually wasted their bullets at an ineffective range, firing prematurely because they confused its appearance in the distance with that of a closer Gotha. British Intelligence, for reasons that are hard to understand, failed to impart the Giants' dimensions: instead of easily correcting this problem, they allowed it to persist.

Despite Britain lacking a Jack to counter the Giants, however, the generals were dismissive of them during and after the war. They were perceived as clumsy and unsophisticated, and flown by inexperienced crews, notions that simply were untrue. Unfair criticism of the Giants extended to the German military too. Major von Bülow deemed the effort that went into their construction and servicing to have been out of proportion to the amount of bombs they dropped on England, and it was conspicuous that the leader of the *Riesenflugzeugen*, von Bentivegni, was never awarded the *Pour le Mérite*, unlike his counterparts in the Naval Airship Division and the England Squadron. If the London raids were a 'strategic propaganda weapon' intended to destroy the spirit and morale of Britain in the first instance, and disrupt British war production in the second, the six aeroplanes available to Rfa 501 at any one time were too few. The German Army expected too much of the Giants.

CHAPTER 7

Defeat of the Raiders

*We were overcome with grief. There was not one among us, whether he
was an officer, a petty officer or an able seaman, who did not feel
that Strasser's death left a yawning gulf that nothing could fill. We no
longer took the same interest in flying; for the spark which Peter had
kindled in ourbreasts had been extinguished.*
Horst von Buttlar in *Zeppelins Over England*, on the
loss of Peter Strasser, 5 August 1918.

If 1917 had been a poor year for the Naval Airship Division, 1918 was to prove
worse. In the first week, on 5 January, a fire raged through the sheds at Ahlhorn, in
northern Germany, destroying four of the newest Navy Zeppelins and razing the
airship base to the ground. The loss of L46, L47, L51 and L58, along with SL20,
was a body blow to the Division and greatly diminished the Zeppelin threat to
Britain. But the raids did not cease quite yet. On the night of 12/13 March five Navy
Zeppelins attacked the Midlands, killing one person in Yorkshire. They might have
taken more lives, but thick cloud led them off course; as it was, the cloud also
obscured them, preventing any sightings and hiding them from roving British
aeroplanes. The following evening, three Zeppelins once again targeted the
Midlands, but were recalled by Strasser when strong north-easterly winds were
forecast. *Kapitänleutnant* Martin Dietrich, commanding L42, however, was close to
the English coast and decided to press on. He paused at sea while darkness fell, then
proceeded inland and bombed West Hartlepool's docks. Eight were killed and thirty-

*The bombers bombed: smoke billows from 'Toska' shed at Tondern, after a
raid by Sopwith Camels from the British aircraft carrier HMS* Furious, *19
July 1918. The two Zeppelins in the shed, L54 and L60, were both destroyed.*
Imperial War Museum

nine injured. A month later, on 12/13 April, five Zeppelins returned to the Midlands. The raid resulted in seven dead and twenty injured, most of the German bombs falling in the countryside rather than on towns or cities. The heights that protected the airships from AA and fighters impeded their navigation and aim.

On 10 May the German Navy was unlucky to lose L62, which blew up while on reconnaissance over the North Sea. The loss of L54 and L60 on 19 July, however, was attributable to British initiative. In the early hours seven Sopwith Camels had taken off from the British aircraft carrier HMS *Furious* and attacked the airship base at Tondern in Schleswig-Holstein, close to Denmark, destroying the two Zeppelins in their shed. Of the British pilots, one fell in the sea, four were forced to land in Denmark as they ran out of fuel and two made it back to HMS *Furious*. Regardless of these setbacks, Strasser remained encouraged by the minor successes of the spring and decided to take part personally in a raid on 5 August. Five Zeppelins were involved and Strasser was on board L70, whose commander was the inexperienced *Kapitänleutnant* Johann von Lossnitzer. Of the very latest X class, this was L70's maiden flight. The colossal Zeppelin measured nearly 2,250,000ft³ and was 700ft long. Powered by seven Maybach engines, it had a top speed of 80mph and could carry over 8,000lb of bombs.

Naval Zeppelin L70 was the most advanced airship of the war and was on its maiden mission when it was destroyed by Major Egbert Cadbury and Captain Robert Leckie, on 5 August 1918. Its commander was **Kapitänleutnant** *Johann von Lossnitzer. Here, the Zeppelin is shown at Friedrichshafen the previous month.* **Imperial War Museum**

L70 and the others arrived within sight of the Norfolk coast soon after 8.00 pm. It is likely that Strasser had been expecting cloud cover across central England to spread eastwards and hide them while there was still daylight, but it was clear out at sea and the Zeppelins were spotted. British airmen were quickly in the air. Among the first up from Great Yarmouth was pilot Major Egbert Cadbury (who had earlier in the war helped to destroy L21) and gunner Captain Robert Leckie (who, in a Flying Boat, had helped to destroy L22 in April 1917). They were in a DH4, a formidable aeroplane with a 375hp Rolls-Royce engine capable of up to 123mph and a ceiling of 22,000ft. They were slow to ascend, despite jettisoning their two bombs, but by 10.10 pm they were at 16,400ft, a thousand feet below L70. They flew head-on at the Zeppelin, which could not see them against the background of thickening cloud. Leckie shot at the nose and then at a point to the rear of the Zeppelin's hull. Before the airship had time to respond and ascend to safety, the explosive bullets tore open the fabric and fire spread along the sides. At the same time Lieutenant R E Keys and his gunner, Air Mechanic A T Harman, in another DH4, were firing at the airship's stern, setting that ablaze. Whichever of the two was the more responsible for the kill – only Cadbury and Leckie received the credit – L70 was split in two and fell seawards off Wells-next-the-Sea. 'It looked like a huge sun,' *Kapitänleutnant* Michael

von Freudenreich on board L63 commented afterwards. 'She went down like a burning arrow.' So perished the Leader of Airships and the inspiration for many of the air raids on Britain, his fiery end guaranteeing him immortality. Twenty-one others had the honour, or misfortune, of dying with him.

Another Zeppelin, L65 (*Kapitänleutnant* Walter Dose) was shot at that night and was lucky not to be brought down with punctured gas cells. All four raiders witnessed the fate of L70 and left for Germany in haste. They climbed to their maximum altitudes and dropped all their bombs. These fell safely out at sea, although some airship commanders wrongly believed they were above land and had dropped them on coastal towns and ports. Had Strasser been a little more cautious, or had he the good fortune to come within sight of land elsewhere along the coast and encountered squadrons equipped with lesser aircraft than DH4s, he might have

Fregattenkäpitan *Peter Strasser,* *wearing the* **Pour le Mérite** *awarded him by Admiral Scheer in September 1917. The driving force of the Naval Airship Division, he perished on board L70.* Imperial War Museum

Naval Zeppelin L53. Commanded by Kapitänleutnant der Reserve *Eduard Prölss, it was shot down on patrol over the North Sea by Flight Sub-Lieutenant Stuart Culley on the morning of 11 August 1918. It was the last German airship to be destroyed in combat.* Imperial War Museum

avoided catastrophe. British Home Defence squadrons, searchlights and AA stretched in an unbroken line along east coast, but the defences were not impervious, even if they now seemed to be. Fortunately for Britain, no further trial was made of them. Strasser's loss to the Naval Airship Division was irreparable and his was the last ever air raid on Britain in the First World War. If the vulnerability of the Zeppelin needed to be underlined, it was done so less than a week later, when, on 11 August, L53, commanded by *Kapitänleutnant der Reserve* Eduard Prölss, was felled off the Dutch coast by Flight Sub-Lieutenant Stuart Douglas Culley, flying a Sopwith Camel.

Flight Sub-Lieutenant Stuart Culley. He took off in a Sopwith Camel from the short deck of a lighter, towed by the destroyer HMS *Redoubt. It took him an hour to climb as high as the unsuspecting L53 and he met no resistance when he fired at it.* Imperial War Museum

German aeroplanes were too busy on the Western Front during the Spring Offensive to resume their attacks on Britain; all the urban centres bombed by Giants at this time were French – Abbeville, Calais, Boulogne and Rouen. By the summer, when a resumption was considered, Germany had developed the Elektron magnesium bomb, an awesome incendiary device that burned at over 1,000° C and could not be put out with water, which would only intensify the fire. Weighing only 1kg (2.2lb) each, these could have been dropped in their thousands. However, in August 1918 the German Army was faltering on the Western Front and the High Command feared bitter reprisals by the allies if they used them at this late hour. Their planned deployment against London was therefore cancelled, but only just in time – an hour before the Gothas were due to set off.

While German air raids abated, it was time for Britain to seek its revenge. Throughout the war members of the public had called for retaliation against Germany, but the authorities had resisted counter-raids, considering them a wasteful diversion of the limited number of aeroplanes at their disposal, all of which were badly needed on the Western Front. What few raids were carried out were tactical in scope rather than strategic. An attempt was made by the RNAS to develop a more ambitious programme of bombing German targets when it established No. 3 Wing, based at Luxeuil, near Nancy in eastern France. The squadron, using Sopwith 1½ Strutter and Short Bomber aeroplanes, hoped to have thirty-five aeroplanes by July 1916, but when it was about to commence operations the RFC commander in France, General Sir Hugh Trenchard, requested some of the Royal Navy's planes in order to maintain British air effectiveness further north. The Somme offensive was about to begin and the RFC had fewer machines than they needed because French manufacturers had failed to supply them with enough engines. The Royal Navy responded generously, but at the expense of the bomber squadron. When the Luxeuil squadron was back up to strength again – in October – several raids were carried out until the end of the year. These included attacks on the Mauser factory at Oberndorf in a combined operation with French aeroplanes, the furnace of the Thyssen Works at Hagendingen, steel works at Volklingen and blast furnaces at St Ingbert. In spring 1917 the Luxeuil wing was broken up.

General Trenchard continued to oppose using any of his resources for anything other than front-line tactical work, but pressure on the British government at home forced it to consider the strategic bombing of Germany more seriously. The South African politician, Lieutenant General Jan Christian Smuts, led a committee looking into Home Defence and air warfare and recommended the creation of an air force independent of the RFC in order to carry out such counter-bombing. He also advised the amalgamation of the RFC and RNAS for air power to be fully effective. Subsequently, the Royal Air Force was formed in early 1918 with Trenchard as Chief of the Air Staff; as a separate unit the Independent Air Force (IAF) was formed on 8 June with the specific remit of carrying out air raids, and a hundred Handley Page V/1500 night bombers were ordered for its ten squadrons. With four engines, six crew and a massive payload, these were Britain's reply to the Giants and they were dubbed 'Bloody Paralysers'. In the spring and summer of the final year of the war DH4s for daytime raiding and Handley Pages for night-time sorties bombed Saarbrücken, Koblenz, Frankfurt, Bonn, Karlsruhe, Trier and Mannheim in Germany, in addition to towns in occupied Belgium and France. In one of the most

A British heavy bomber: the Handley Page V/1500, nicknamed the 'Bloody Paralyser'. Only three were ready for use before the Armistice. Imperial War Museum

spectacular air raids, on 18 May 1918, thirty-three British aeroplanes bombed Cologne, causing widespread damage and killing 110 civilians. At the close of war when Austria-Hungary had surrendered there were plans afoot to move the IAF to Prague and bomb Berlin from there. Trenchard made arrangements for a reconnaissance of the Czech city and for a trainload of supplies to precede the bombers' flight there, but the Armistice rendered the action unnecessary. Still, by the end, Allied air raids on Germany had killed 746 and injured 1,843. The number of daylight raids carried out on enemy soil had tripled in the course of four years of war and the night-time figure had risen from seven in 1914 to 234 in 1918.

These air raids compelled the Germans to do what the British had done previously, that is to divert fighter aircraft, searchlights, AA batteries and machine guns away from the front line in France and Belgium, and to defend deep in their own country. Piecemeal protective measures were reorganized, and balloon and kite barrages similar to those in London were erected in the Saar valley to protect the chemical, powder and explosives factories there. German officials enjoined the populace in affected towns and cities to pay no attention to the raids, but the public

Aftermath of a raid on Germany, 18 February 1918: damage at Trier. **Royal Air Force Museum**

reacted exactly as they had in Britain: many of them panicked. Vulnerability to air attack was just as frightening and demoralizing to Teutons as it was to Anglo-Saxons. The major difference between the two countries was that Germany suffered the effects for a shorter time than her cousin, and because of her larger geographical spread, experienced less nationwide disruption to production.

*

The impact of four years of intermittent air raids on British war production was significant, even though few factories received bomb damage or staff were killed. Seventy-five per cent of munitions workers stopped work during raids, and it has been estimated that the production of munitions suffered a loss of one-sixth during the war as a result. Steel works managers found that the morning after a raid as few as ten per cent of their employees would turn up on time and twenty per cent would not come in at all. This not only slowed down production but also meant that vital metal was wasted; what is more, unattended blast furnaces risked breakdown and even explosion. Disruption to the railways caused by blackouts only exacerbated industrial problems, delaying the transportation of raw materials and finished goods. The fact that many of these disturbances were the result of false alarms is not an issue – imagined raids could be just as disruptive as actual ones. When a phantom Zeppelin was seen off Scarborough on 10 February 1916, for example, railway lights were extinguished at places as far away as Bath, Worcester and Nottingham, factories stopped production as far afield as Gloucester and whole swathes of the countryside were plunged into darkness.

Countering the air raids meant diverting badly needed aircraft and their pilots and attendant mechanics away from the front lines, along with other war matériel and personnel. At their peak, Home Defence personnel numbered a total of 17,341, while at the beginning of 1918 469 AA guns, 622 searchlights, 258 height-finders, ten sound locators and up to 376 aeroplanes were based in Britain for its defence. The manpower required to train and produce these, in addition to building stations and aerodromes, was considerable. The German air attacks also consumed the time and personnel of the police force, fire brigade, ambulance and telephone services. Along with rebuilding and repair, the material cost of the raids was expensive.

As the most profound effect of the bombing was psychological, undermining morale and the nation's will to fight, it was a price well worth paying. Although some in the military regarded the air raid attacks on Britain as a sideshow unworthy of serious attention, politicians recognized the need to bolster public confidence by strengthening Home Defences. Had they neglected this they might have lost popular support for the war effort, which was essential for victory. However, their success in maintaining British spirits is as much about German failure in crushing them. Although the enemy was one step ahead of the British throughout the war – the British defences constantly had to catch up and adapt to new threats posed by the Zeppelin 'height climbers', Gothas and Giants – Germany failed to press home the advantage each time it had it. Earlier in the conflict, for example, the Kaiser's reluctance to sanction the bombing campaign meant that Britain was not attacked in 1914 when its defences were weakest and its public were least mentally and physically prepared. Later on, the Germans may be criticized for giving too much priority to raiding London. As the heavily populated capital city, it was a natural target, not least for propaganda purposes, but once its defences were in place the German airships would have had more success assaulting the helpless industrial cities of the North and Midlands. This might have stretched Britain's capacity to cope with bombs and with popular unrest to breaking point, especially if the Naval Airship Division and the German Army had co-operated and concentrated their attacks in bigger, more devastating raids that would have been less easy to repulse. But they did not. Although they damaged morale, the raids were too few ever to break Britain's will altogether, and in the long run the anger they caused actually strengthened British determination to carry on fighting.

The airship raids resulted in the deaths of some 560 and injured nearly 1,400; sorties by aeroplanes accounted for a further 857 dead and at least 2,000 other casualties. In total, therefore, the air offensive against Britain in the First World War claimed the lives of more than 1,400, and injured another 3,500. Tragically, in London twenty-four of the dead and 196 of the injured were the result of anti-aircraft fire. Twenty-eight British airmen lost their lives defending the nation; the Germans lost 158 airship crewmen and fifty-seven Gotha crewmen (excluding

OUR FRIEND THE ENEMY.

JOHN BULL (*very calmly*). "AH, HERE HE COMES AGAIN—MY BEST RECRUITER."

Punch, *October 1915.* Punch Publications

accidental casualties returning home) attacking it. The damage caused was valued at £3,000,000, and in the London area alone some 12,000 premises were either damaged or destroyed. These figures are minor in comparison with the scale of death and destruction on the Western Front and elsewhere in the war; the number of casualties is also small compared with those killed by the Spanish flu epidemic that ravaged war-weakened Europe immediately after the Armistice. The significance of the air raid casualties, however, is that they were predominantly civilian. For the first time in centuries the British public experienced conflict at home, and the sea, which, as Shakespeare wrote, served the country 'in the office of a wall', had been overcome. The air raids were a new form of warfare and a terrifying one: the outrage and distress they caused should not be underestimated.

The war's end banished the spectre of further raids, but only for a time of course. In a little over two decades air raids would erupt on Britain on a scale and with a ferocity unimaginable in 1918.

Gazetteer

This section is intended to provide useful information regarding the cities, towns and other places relevant to the German air raids of the First World War. It offers a selection of sites, chosen because of their historical significance or because there is something tangible for the reader to see and visit, such as artefacts in a museum. Particular attention has been made to include memorials commemorating the air raids of the Great War, many of which have fallen into obscurity and are in danger of being lost to the public, as well as examples of air raid damage that are still visible. The gazetteer is divided into several sections: London, England (excluding London), and Scotland. For convenience, London itself is subdivided into Central and Greater London, and England is subdivided into counties (although not all counties are included). The space devoted to the capital reflects its strategic importance and the fact that the raiders so often made it their target.

Although not a comprehensive guide, for reasons of space, it should nevertheless be remembered that the air raids affected all areas of Britain in the First World War. Not only were towns and cities attacked the length and breadth of the country, but places that escaped bombing lived under the threat of attack and experienced disruption as a result of alarms and rumoured sightings.

One final point: in the case of museum collections, readers are reminded that exhibits are not guaranteed to be always on display.

German cartoon, from Lustige Blätter. *At night in Trafalgar Square, a police officer asks the nation's hero,* 'God damn, Mister Nelson, what are you looking for down here?' Nelson replies, 'Well, just you spend some time up there with the threat of a Zeppelin!'

LONDON

CENTRAL LONDON

Albert Memorial, Kensington Gardens

This imposing monument by George Gilbert Scott was erected in memory of Prince Albert, the Prince Consort of Queen Victoria. During the First World War bright gilding was removed from the huge statue of Albert, as well as from the figures and decorations of the canopy and flèche. The official reason for this was to reduce the monument's visibility, lest it assist a German raider to target Kensington Palace, a third of a mile to the west. However, it may also have been done in order to downplay the Royal family's German connections – Albert of Saxe-Coburg-Gotha was, of course, German, and Kaiser Wilhelm II, as the grandson of Victoria and Albert, was cousin to the then reigning British king, George V. The gilding was finally reinstated as part of major restoration work by English Heritage, completed in 1998.

The nearest Tube stations to the Albert Memorial are Queensway and Lancaster Gate on the Central Line, and High Street Kensington on the District and Circle Lines.

Bedford Hotel, Bloomsbury

On the night of 24/25 September 1917, during one of the earliest night raids carried out by Gothas, and at the start of the 'harvest moon offensive', visitors from out of

Bedford Hotel, Bloomsbury. A 50kg (110lb) bomb, dropped by a Gotha on 24 September 1917, exploded outside killing thirteen hotel guests and staff who were watching the raid. Another twenty-two persons were injured. Imperial War Museum

town less used to the spectacle of air raids were standing on the steps of the old Bedford Hotel, along with members of the hotel staff. While they watched the roving searchlights and listened to the rattle of anti-aircraft fire, a 50kg (110lb) bomb fell several feet away in the road. It blew them to pieces, smashed the hotel railings, shattered the windows and threw guests inside across their rooms and down stairs 'like the leaves of a tree in a storm', as one description put it. Thirteen were killed by the blast and twenty-two were injured. The thirteen Gothas raiding the capital that night claimed a total of twenty-one lives and injured over seventy.

The Bedford Hotel still exists, though a modern building has replaced the earlier one. Outside, on the forecourt wall, next to the car park entrance, a plaque remembers the air raid and those who perished here.

The Bedford Hotel is halfway down Southampton Row; the nearest London Underground Station is Russell Square on the Piccadilly Line to the north; Holborn Station on the Piccadilly and Central Lines is a slightly further walk to the south.

See the entry for Piccadilly, regarding the same raid.

Brompton Cemetery, Chelsea
Reginald Warneford VC, the first British pilot to shoot down a German airship, the Army Zeppelin LZ37, was given a public funeral in Brompton Cemetery on 22 June 1915. His handsome grave monument reads: 'Flight Sub-Lieutenant Reginald Alexander John Warneford VC, RNAS. Born 15 Oct. 1891, accidentally killed 17 June 1915'. Above this inscription there is a wreathed portrait of the fallen hero, smiling benignly and in uniform. The words 'courage', 'initiative' and 'intrepidity' accompany the portrait; the pediment is decorated with a stone representation of Warneford's Victoria Cross.

Below the dedication, a relief dramatically depicts the Zeppelin exploding above the Belgian countryside while Warneford's Morane-Saulnier aeroplane soars skyward. Beneath this there is a further inscription, informing the visitor that the gravestone was 'Erected by readers of the *Daily Express* to commemorate the heroic exploit in destroying a Zeppelin airship near Ghent on June 7 1915'.

The heart of Brompton Cemetery is dominated by the Great Circle: Warneford's monument is located at the northern end of the Colonnade leading to this. He is buried in the second row on the eastern side of the Central Avenue, and the ashes of his eldest sister, Gladys, rest with him. The northern entrance to the Cemetery is on Old Brompton Road, the southern is on Fulham Road. The closest London Underground stations are, respectively, West Brompton and Fulham Broadway. Both are on the District Line to and from Wimbledon.

See the entry for Highworth, Wiltshire.

The memorial in Brompton Cemetery to Flight Sub-Lieutenant Reginald Warneford VC. He was the first pilot to destroy a German airship, Army Zeppelin LZ37.

The pavement beside Cleopatra's Needle on Victoria Embankment, ruptured by a 50kg (110lb) explosive during the first night raid on London by Gothas, 4/5 September 1917. Passengers on a tram and passers-by were caught in the blast: three died, six were injured. Damage to the pedestals and the bronze sphinx in the photograph is still evident today. Imperial War Museum

Cleopatra's Needle, Victoria Embankment

Just before midnight on 4/5 September 1917 one of four bombs aimed by a Gotha at Charing Cross Station fell on the Victoria Embankment, a few feet away from Cleopatra's Needle. A tramcar was passing just at the moment of the explosion, crowded with passengers. The conductor and two of the passengers, a man and a woman, were fatally wounded and another nine were seriously hurt. A ruptured gas main beneath the shattered road was fortunate not to blow up. Cleopatra's Needle was damaged by shrapnel. The raid on London, conducted by ten Gothas, provoked a reshuffle of the city's defences. Barrage balloons were instigated and sound-location posts established to track the German aeroplanes' movements.

A bronze plaque on the plinth of the right-hand sphinx flanking Cleopatra's Needle records the incident in what it erroneously refers to as the first raid by aeroplanes on London: it was actually the first *night-time* raid on the capital by aeroplanes. The pedestal of the obelisk and the plinths bearing the sphinxes still clearly bear the scars caused by the explosion; holes in the right-hand sphinx show where bomb fragments punctured the thick bronze sculpture.

Cleopatra's Needle is located next to the Thames, halfway between Hungerford and Waterloo bridges. Opposite it, incidentally, is a large stone and bronze Great War monument presented 'to the British nation from the grateful people of Belgium'. The closest Tube station is 200 yards away at Embankment, which is served by the Northern, Bakerloo, District and Circle Lines.

Dolphin public house, Lamb's Conduit Passage, Holborn

On 8 September 1915, after bombing Queen Square and en route to bombing Farringdon Road and Bartholomew Close, *Kapitänleutnant* Mathy in L13 dropped a high explosive outside the entrance to the Dolphin tavern. Henry Coombs who was watching the raid was killed instantly by the blast and the front of the pub was torn out. In Lamb's Conduit Passage, house fires were started at numbers 7 and 10, and Fireman Green suffered fatal burns while helping to put them out. He was posthumously awarded the Silver Medal of the London County Council for his brave conduct.

The Dolphin itself is still open, standing on the corner of Lamb's Conduit Passage and Red Lion Street. A clock hanging on one of the walls when the raid occurred stopped at 10.49 pm, the exact time of the explosion. It has never been restarted and it still shows the moment when time stood still, high on the wall to the left of the bar; an explanatory notice is below it.

The nearest London Underground station is Holborn on the Central and Piccadilly Lines.

See the entries for Queen Square, Farringdon Road and the Museum of London.

Naval Zeppelin L13 which, under the command of **Kapitänleutnant Mathy,** *inflicted widespread destruction in central London on the night of 8/9 September 1915. The damage was estimated at over £500,000, the highest for any single raid of the First World War.* Imperial War Museum

The plaque outside 61 Farringdon Road, which was rebuilt in 1917.

Farringdon Road, Clerkenwell

The premises at 61 Farringdon Road was one of many destroyed by *Kapitänleutnant* Mathy in L13 on the night of 8/9 September 1915. The bomb that fell here occurred in between those dropped on the Dolphin tavern in Lamb's Conduit Street and Bartholomew Close. Subsequent devices started fires in City warehouses and resulted in over £500,000 material damage. This was the worst for any single raid in the Great War and accounted for nearly a fifth of the total air raid damage to Britain.

61 Farringdon Road was rebuilt in 1917. A white metal plaque with black lettering still records its destruction by a Zeppelin.

The property is situated close to Farringdon Underground station, on the District and Circle and Metropolitan Lines.

See the entries for Queen Square, the Dolphin public house in Lamb's Conduit Passage, and the Museum of London.

Imperial War Museum, Lambeth

The Imperial War Museum contains numerous important items relating to air raids on Britain in the First World War. Perhaps the most impressive examples – certainly the largest – are to be found in the atrium, which is used to showcase exhibits such as aeroplanes and tanks. Displayed here is an observation car from a Zeppelin. The object, which is streamlined and finned and looks suspiciously like a huge bomb, in fact contained an airman who, with nerves of steel, was lowered thousands of feet by cable to trail below the Zeppelin. This enabled the airship to peer beneath clouds while remaining above them and out of sight, the observer being in contact with the main craft by telephone. This particular observation car fell from Army Zeppelin LZ90 and landed near Mistley, Essex, on the night of 2/3 September 1916, during the raid in which William Leefe Robinson VC shot down SL11. It had been lowered unmanned when the winch went out of control and was recovered virtually intact. LZ90 bombed Haverhill, Essex, before returning to Germany, probably missing the destruction of SL11.

Higher up in the atrium is suspended a Sopwith Camel 2F1, a type of Camel developed by the RNAS to provide a defence for the Fleet against enemy Zeppelins, and which could take off from early aircraft carriers. This particular one (No. N6812) was flown by Flight Sub-Lieutenant Stuart Douglas Culley, RAF, on 11 August 1918 when he took off from a ship being towed by the destroyer HMS *Redoubt* near the Dutch coast. Off Terschelling at nearly 19,000ft he brought down L53, commanded by *Kapitänleutnant der Reserve* Prölss. This was the last German airship to be shot down in the war and Culley received the Distinguished Service Order for his action.

Hanging near to Culley's aeroplane is a BE2c that flew with the Home Defence squadrons, while on the upper landing of the atrium there is a British 1-pounder Mark 2 Anti-Aircraft Gun that is held to have been the first gun fired in defence of the City of London. Issued to the AA station at Gresham College, and known since as the 'Gresham Gun', it shot at – and missed – Mathy's L13 on the evening of 8 September 1915. Interestingly, the officer in charge of the gun that night was Sub-

A Zeppelin observation car, used to lower a crewman from the airship to see below cloud cover. This particular one was empty when it fell from German Army Zeppelin LZ90 during a raid on 2/3 September 1916. Recovered in Essex, it is now displayed at the Imperial War Museum. Imperial War Museum

Lieutenant Charles ffoulkes, RNVR, who subsequently became the first curator and Secretary of the Imperial War Museum.

On the lower ground floor of the museum there is a comprehensive series of displays detailing the First World War. One of them deals specifically with the air raids on Britain and contains several interesting items. These include the cap and insignia worn by crew members of Zeppelin L33 (commanded by *Kapitänleutnant der Reserve* Alois Böcker, L33 was brought down in Essex by AA in the early hours of 24 September 1916, and its crew interned), recovered incendiary and high explosive bombs, a large felt boot worn on board Zeppelins, air raid notices and propaganda posters.

Relating to William Leefe Robinson's destruction of SL11 on 3 September 1916 are a fragment of fabric salvaged from the airship, souvenir postcards depicting its destruction, pieces of recovered metal made into souvenirs and sold in aid of the Red Cross and a facsimile of Robinson's letter to a Mrs Wisher, thanking her for her gift of a cigarette case in recognition of his deed. From L31, shot down by Tempest four weeks after SL11, there is the distinguished *Kapitänleutnant* Mathy's bent and twisted binoculars, and a machine gun ammunition box whose intriguing distortion is due to the impact on the bullets it contained. Also exhibited is a model of L33, and on a touch screen monitor visitors may select archive film footage relating to raids by Zeppelins and Gothas.

The Imperial War Museum is on Lambeth Road. The closest Underground station is Lambeth North on the Bakerloo Line.

Inns of Court, Holborn

During the Zeppelin raid on the evening of Wednesday, 13 October 1915, *Kapitänleutnant* Breithaupt in L15 dropped several bombs in and around Lincoln's Inn. One bomb fell next to the seventeenth century Chapel of Lincoln's Inn, shattering windows and damaging the stonework. Another device fell next door in Chancery Lane, where the janitor of Lincoln's Inn, Mr G. P. Brown, was blown to smithereens hurrying home to his sick wife. After finishing with Lincoln's Inn, Breithaupt moved on to nearby Gray's Inn, dropping several incendiary bombs in South Square and on its rooftops. The historic oak-panelled Hall was endangered, but the Inn's own voluntary firemen succeeded in staunching the fire before it could get out of hand. L15 then proceeded further westwards where it encountered Rawlinson's newly-employed French 75mm mobile gun, which helped drive the German raider away.

On the evening of 18 December 1917 a second raid befell Lincoln's Inn, interrupting a Bench Council meeting. Assuring themselves that the Hall wine cellar was bombproof, the Benchers retired there for the duration. While they supped oysters and champagne, a bomb dropped by a German aeroplane landed in Stone Buildings; no one was injured but superficial damage was done outside the Drill Hall to windows, pipes and masonry.

Today, in Lincoln's Inn, a plaque on the north-west corner of the Chapel records the Zeppelin bomb of 13 October 1915 and the time of its explosion, at 9.25 pm; a round stone marks the precise spot where it landed and scars caused by shrapnel may still plainly be seen on the side of the Chapel. A similar plaque remembers the 1917 aeroplane bombing, affixed to what is now the Inns of Court & City Yeomanry

Air raid damage at Gray's Inn, caused by **Kapitänleutnant** *Breithaupt, in* **L15, on 13 October 1915.** Imperial War Museum

Headquarters; the stones and bricks of the surrounding buildings remain pockmarked from the explosion.

The nearest Underground stations to Lincoln's Inn and Gray's Inn are Chancery Lane on the Central Line and Holborn on the Central and Piccadilly Lines.

Liverpool Street station, City

Tragedy struck Liverpool Street station on 13 June 1917 when three bombs dropped by Gothas struck the railway terminus. Two penetrated the arched roof: one was a dud and failed to go off, the other exploded on platform 9. The third hit a passenger train as it was about to depart for Hunstanton in Norfolk, destroying the dining car and setting two coaches alight. Many of the victims were trapped inside, the dead including both railway staff and passengers. Thirteen died altogether, a loss of life which could have been reduced, if not avoided altogether, had the City Police warned the station authorities of the raid and people been advised to take cover. A famous eyewitness to the tragedy, the poet Siegfried Sassoon, was left feeling helpless.

Liverpool Street station was also hit earlier in the war. On 8/9 September 1915

Air raid damage in Liverpool Street. Kapitanleutnant *Mathy, commanding* L13, *aimed four bombs at Liverpool Street railway station on 8/9 September 1915, but only one fell on target, damaging a portion of track. The other three explosives landed in adjacent streets where two buses were hit, killing fifteen of their passengers.* Imperial War Museum

Kapitänleutnant Mathy in L13 dropped bombs on adjoining streets, striking two omnibuses and killing fifteen. Regarding this particular raid, see the entries for Queen Square, the Dolphin public house in Lamb's Conduit Passage and the Museum of London.

Liverpool Street station is much changed and modernized since it was first built in the nineteenth century; still a busy railway station, it lies on the Central, Circle, Hammersmith & City and Metropolitan Lines.

Museum of London, City

The Museum contains few exhibits on the First World War London air raids except for short clips of archive film footage concerning anti-German riots in the capital, and an aircraft recognition poster comparing the silhouettes of British and German airships and aeroplanes. Other aspects of the Great War are better covered, notably women's war work and the contribution this made to women's suffrage: those over thirty years of age finally received the vote after the war was over on account of this.

Just west of the Museum of London is Bartholomew Close. Here, at around 11.00 pm on the evening of 8 September 1915, fell one of several bombs dropped by *Kapitänleutnant* Mathy in L13 (see the entries for Queen Square, the Dolphin public house in Lamb's Conduit Passage and Farringdon Road). This particular bomb weighed 300kg (660lb), making it the largest dropped on Britain so far – it was Mathy's 'Love Gift' to London. Charles Henley was on fire duty in the Close at the time and was preparing to retire for the night in his fire-box when he received a telephone call to remain on duty. Standing outside in the calm autumn evening he heard the whirring sound of the Zeppelin's propellers getting closer, accompanied by the dull thuds of exploding bombs. At that moment two men came out of the Admiral Carter pub – William Fenge, who lived above it, and Frederick Saunders – who had also heard the noise. They decided to run for cover but were too late as a huge explosion rocked the Close. When Henley came round he found the two men from the pub had been killed and the buildings all around were shattered and on fire.

Amid the devastation, a celebrated act of bravery was performed by thirteen-year-old Violet Buckthorpe, who lived at number 21. She rushed upstairs and rescued her two-year-old baby sister, Marjorie, then climbed down the broken stairs into the street. After kneeling down and praying, she hurried to the nearest hospital where the baby was taken care of and where she herself was found to be sorely wounded and bleeding, something she had not noticed in her concern for her sister. For her actions she later received a gold watch and an educational grant for £30.

In 1915 Victorian properties surrounded Bartholomew Close; the disappearance of these is a testimony to the bombing of two world wars and they have been replaced with offices, flats and hospital buildings. The Admiral Carter pub also no longer exists. South of here, however, is Postman's Park, a place of tranquillity formed from three old churchyards, between King Edward Street and St Martin's-le-Grand/Aldersgate Street. Against a wall in the middle there is a national memorial dedicated to heroic men and women who gave their lives for others, which was inaugurated in 1900. Among those celebrated here is Alfred Smith, a

Bartholomew Close following the raid by Kapitänleutnant Mathy on 8/9 September 1915. The explosive that landed here was the first 300kg (660lb) device to be dropped on the country. Mathy termed it his 'Love Gift' to the city. It killed two men who had left a pub to find out what was going on and wrought extensive material damage in the area. Imperial War Museum

policeman who was killed while saving the lives of women and children in an air raid on 13 June 1917 (the day of the Poplar school raid). His tiled plaque is among those on the left.

The Museum of London is situated between Barbican and St Paul's Underground stations, and is not much further from Moorgate. It is clearly signposted from each of these. Barbican Tube station is on the Circle, Metropolitan and Hammersmith & City Lines; St Paul's is on the Central Line; Moorgate is on the Northern, Circle, Metropolitan and Hammersmith & City Lines, and is also a train station.

Odhams Printing Works, Long Acre, Covent Garden

On the night of 28/29 January 1918 some 500 of London's citizens were sheltering from a German aeroplane raid in the basement of Odhams printing works, which, because of its concrete floors, was an official public air raid shelter. Soon after midnight a 300kg (660lb) bomb dropped by a Giant aeroplane, R12, exploded just outside in the street. Although the building largely withstood the initial blast, a fire broke out in the paper store and before all those inside could escape by the single remaining exit the floors above them collapsed. Thirty-eight were burned or crushed to death and another eighty-five were seriously burned and injured; two-thirds of the victims were either women or children. No single bomb falling on London in the First World War caused more casualties. A journalist described the grisly scene early the next morning:

> *The wrecked printing works is a frightful spectacle, it has been so inhumanely mangled – if I may use the expression – by the bomb. A German explosive is not content with killing human beings and demolishing buildings; it also hacks and gashes, making*

The basement of Odhams Printing Works. It was from here that most of the building's thirty-eight dead were recovered. Imperial War Museum

everything it destroys a horror to look at. When I got to the place, the ruins were still being searched for bodies. I saw some brought out. They were maimed and distorted almost beyond identification.

The printing works stood on the corner of Long Acre and Endell Street, and was bounded by Arne Street. A modern office block now occupies the site. A short passage called Odhams Walk, which runs through the apartment complex and shops on the other corner of Endell Street, commemorates the press but it does not mark its location.

A short walk away in Covent Garden is St Paul's Church, whose rector in the First World War was the Reverend Edward Mosse. He was a familiar figure in the area and would go into the streets during air raids to shepherd people to safety. It was 'while ministering to his people' that he came to be among those killed in the Odhams explosion. He is remembered by a bronze tablet on a doorway on the northern side of the Church, facing the gate into the Market; a stone cross, inscribed 1914-1918, is on the wall above it.

Covent Garden is the nearest Underground station, on the Piccadilly Line.

Piccadilly, Mayfair

The Royal Academy of Art on Piccadilly was hit during the first of the 'harvest moon' raids, on 24 September 1917. On this particular night three Gothas attacked London, while others of the England Squadron bombed Dover and other targets in

Royal Academy, No. 9 Gallery. This was shattered by a 50kg (110lb) bomb from a Gotha, 24 September 1917. Imperial War Museum

Kent; a total of twenty-one persons were killed and seventy injured. The 50kg (110lb) bomb that landed on the Royal Academy of Art fell through the glass roof of No. 9 Gallery and blew a hole through into basement; no one was hurt but some statues were damaged.

A black roundel is inscribed in commemoration of the raid, set into the right-hand side of the marble doorway leading from the Lecture Room to No. 9 Gallery. Visitors should note that shrapnel damaged the marble that surrounds the inscription. Although access to the Lecture Room and No. 9 Gallery is usually by paying admission to an exhibition, a polite request at the Information desk to view the memorial should gain entrance for that purpose.

Along from the Royal Academy of Art is Piccadilly Circus where a high explosive bomb weighing 300kg (660lb) fell outside Swan & Edgar's shop at 11.30pm on 19 October 1917, during the 'Silent Raid'. The bomb was released by L45, one of the 'height climber' Zeppelins intending to bomb the Midlands that night, but which was blown off course by a gale over London. The commander, *Kapitänleutnant* Kölle, was able to release several bombs on the metropolis before the wind carried the Zeppelin southwards and away. The one beside Piccadilly Circus killed seven, seriously injured nine and wounded many others. If the bomb had fallen earlier in the evening when the streets were much busier, the number of fatalities would have been considerably worse. The blast caused a crater 9ft deep and 10ft wide in the road, blowing in shop-fronts and smashing windows. Dozens more were killed and hurt in Camberwell and Lewisham in south-east London by the other bombs dropped by Kölle that night.

The Royal Academy of Art lies between Piccadilly Circus Underground station, on the Piccadilly and Bakerloo Lines, and Green Park on the Jubilee, Piccadilly and Victoria Lines.

For the 'harvest moon' raids, see the entry for the Bedford Hotel, Bloomsbury. For Kölle's earlier adventures during the 'Silent Raid', see the entry for Northampton.

Queen Square, Bloomsbury

Queen Square was one of several sites hit in the raid of 8/9 September 1915 when *Kapitänleutnant* Mathy sowed death and destruction across Bloomsbury, Holborn and the City. His Zeppelin, L13, making its fourth raid on England, was plainly visible that clear night – so clear some eyewitnesses even claimed they could make out the crew members on board. The spectacle of the raider, the beams of the searchlights, fires and explosions made a deep impression upon the hundreds of thousands of onlookers. One American journalist captured the scene:

> *Seven million people of the biggest city in the world stand gazing into the sky from the darkened streets. Here is the climax to the twentieth century! It is dull yellow – the colour of the harvest moon. The long fingers of searchlights, reaching up from the roof of the city, are touching all sides of the death messenger with their white tips. Great booming sounds shake the city. They are Zeppelin bombs – falling – killing – burning. Lesser noises, of shooting, are nearer at hand, the noise of aerial guns sending shrapnel into the sky... Suddenly you realize that the biggest city in the world has become the night battlefield on which seven million harmless men, women and children live.*

A bronze plate records the raid and marks the spot where Mathy's bomb exploded; its faded inscription is set in the middle of a circle of crazy paving, in the northern half of the Square's garden. Because the high explosive bomb exploded near the centre of the Square and away from the surrounding houses and hospital buildings, which included the Alexandra Hospital for Children (now Alexandra House), windows were shattered but no one was injured.

Queen Square is five minutes walk from Russell Square Underground Station on the Piccadilly Line.

See the entries for the Dolphin public house in Lamb's Conduit Passage, Farringdon Road and the Museum of London.

Royal Hospital Chelsea

The Royal Hospital Chelsea, designed by Sir Christopher Wren, was founded in the late seventeenth century by Charles II to provide relief for aged and invalided veterans of the army. The Royal Hospital has provided a place of retirement for army veterans ever since. As such, one might have expected its occupants to have seen the last of the horrors of conflict. Unfortunately, that has not always been so. The North-

The North-East Wing of the Royal Hospital Chelsea, ripped apart by the first 1,000kg (2,200lb) bomb dropped on the country, 16 February 1918. Five people died in the explosion. Rebuilt after the First World War, the same building was destroyed a second time in 1945 by a V2 rocket. Imperial War Museum

East Wing of the Royal Hospital has fared badly in not just one world war, but two. In the first instance, it was destroyed on the evening of 16 February 1918 by a 1,000kg (2,200lb) bomb, delivered by Giant R39. The device, the first of its weight to be dropped on Britain, killed an officer of the hospital staff, his wife, two sons and a niece. Remarkably, three other children were recovered alive from the rubble.

After the war the North-East Wing was rebuilt in 1921 in its original form. It was then destroyed for a second time on 3 January 1945 by a German V2 rocket, leaving another five dead and nineteen injured. It was rebuilt again in 1965 and was reopened in January 1966 by the Prime Minister, Harold Wilson.

Looking closely at the North-East Wing, today, one can see that the bricks used in its reconstruction are a shade lighter than those of the seventeenth century original parts. Otherwise it adheres strictly to Wren's design. A grey stone tablet detailing the tragic history of the building has been placed on one of its walls (although the text mistakenly refers to the First World War bomb as being 500lb).

The North-East Wing and the stone tablet are close to the east gate of the Royal Hospital, which also gives access to the Museum. Members of the public are welcome daily, although the hours of access to the Museum and the rest of the Royal Hospital (the splendid Chapel and Hall are especially popular) are restricted. Next to the Royal Hospital is the National Army Museum, which has extensive collections relating to the First World War and is also well worth a visit.

Royal Hospital Chelsea faces on to Royal Hospital Road. The closest Tube station is half a mile away at Sloane Square, on the District and Circle Line. Signs direct visitors from there to the Hospital.

St Edmund the King & Martyr Church, City

The church of St Edmund the King & Martyr on Lombard Street was devastated on the morning of 7 July 1917 in the second daylight raid on London by Gothas. The England Squadron took advantage of improved weather over the North Sea and the recall of Nos. 56 and 66 Squadrons to France, and inflicted fifty-four deaths and 190 injured (although ten of the dead and over one quarter of the wounded were attributable to falling AA). Twenty-one of the German bombers had approached the capital parallel with the Thames, swung up through Essex and the northern limits of London, then wheeled round before Hendon and crossed the metropolis in a south-east direction. There was a heavy concentration of bombs in the City – ones near to Lombard Street falling in Moorgate and three in Fenchurch Street. The high explosive which landed on St Edmund's at 10.00 am broke the main beam of the roof, necessitating its replacement and the restoration of the whole church. St Edmund's did not reopen until 1 October 1919, and suffered later indignity in the Second World War, when incendiaries damaged it in 1941.

Rusted and twisted fragments of the 1917 bomb survive in a glass case; these are usually on display inside the church, but while St Edmund's undergoes modern restoration the offending item is being kept along the road at St Mary Woolnoth's where it may be seen on request.

St Edmund's is a short walk from Bank and Monument stations on the London Underground, served, respectively, by the Central and Northern, and District and Circle Lines.

St Pancras Station, Camden

Following the night of 16/17 February 1918, in which the Royal Hospital Chelsea was hit, one of the Giants involved in that raid returned to London the next night on a solo mission. Commanded by *Leutnant* Borchers, R25 dropped bombs across the city, releasing its final stack of eight 50kg (110lb) high explosives on St Pancras railway station and the Midland Grand Hotel. One exploded on the steps of the station abutting Euston Road, another dislodged two pinnacles from the top of the hotel tower and smashed through the glass-roofed carriageway to explode among people below. This caused the most casualties and wrecked the booking hall, first-class waiting room and ground floor of the hotel. Another bomb fell outside the station where it damaged a public house and a woodshed, killing the woodchopper and his dog. The total of those killed was twenty-one, with twenty-two injured. Rescuing survivors inside the station was hampered by the failure of the electric lights.

The station has changed little over the years since the damage was put right and the exterior of the hotel has been restored recently to its full Victorian Gothic splendour, as designed by George Gilbert Scott. Standing next to St Pancras on Euston Road is King's Cross, the station from which Mrs Morrison-Bell and others watched one of the 'harvest moon' Gotha raids in the autumn of 1917. The arches where she stood at the front of the station, however, are now obscured by a modern extension containing a ticket office and fast food outlets.

St Pancras and King's Cross share a London Underground station, which is on the Northern, Piccadilly, Circle, Victoria, Hammersmith & City and Metropolitan Lines.

Strand theatres, Aldwych

The bombs from a Zeppelin that fell here on the evening of 13 October 1915 aroused two contrasting responses in the packed theatres of the area – panic and fortitude. *Kapitänleutnant* Breithaupt, L15, had aimed his series of high explosives and incendiaries at the Admiralty, off Trafalgar Square, but, due to the forward momentum of the Zeppelin, these fell half a mile off target in the Strand and Aldwych, two of the busiest thoroughfares in the capital. One device struck the rear of the Lyceum Theatre in Exeter Street, showering glass into the auditorium; another blew a hole in Wellington Street, killing seventeen and setting alight a gas main; another fell outside the entrance to the Strand Theatre; and one fell outside the Waldorf Hotel. The performance of a drama, *Between Two Women*, at the Lyceum was abandoned in a hurry. At the Strand, where Fred Terry and Julia Neilson were starring in *The Scarlet Pimpernel*, a Russian member of the orchestra became hysterical at the sound of the bombs crashing outside and insisted he had been killed, but Fred Terry came on stage to restore audience nerves with a patriotic sing-along. Across the road, at the Gaiety where George Grossmith and James Blakeley were appearing in a musical comedy, both players and audience ignored altogether the blasts and bangs from the street. They did not emerge until after the final curtain, when they found the road in ruins and corpses in the street. L15, after proceeding eastwards and bombing the Inns of Court, was long gone.

The Lyceum Theatre is situated next to the corner of Wellington Street and the Strand; the Strand Theatre is nearby on Aldwych, next to the Waldorf Hotel. The Gaiety closed in 1939, but a plaque marking its site may be found on a building

Wellington Street, after the Zeppelin raid of 13/14 October 1915. One of several bombs dropped in the area by **Kapitanleutnant** *Breithaupt, in L15, detonated here, killing seventeen people in the street and igniting a gas main.* Imperial War Museum

nearly opposite the entrance to Somerset House. The area is a busy bus route and is within easy walking distance of several London Underground stations. The nearest is Temple Station on the District and Circle Lines.

*   *   *

GREATER LONDON

Alkham Road, Stoke Newington

16 Alkham Road has the unenviable distinction of being the first place in London to have been hit in an air raid, on 31 May 1915. The enemy airman responsible was *Hauptmann* Erich Linnarz, the commander of Army Zeppelin LZ38.

The occupants of the house at that time were Mr and Mrs Lovell and their children; that night they also had two female visitors staying upstairs. These were roused from their slumbers shortly after 11.00 pm when an incendiary dropped by the Zeppelin bounced off the neighbour's chimney and lodged itself in the rafters of the Lovells' roof, setting the upper bedroom on fire. Fortunately, Mr Lovell was able to rescue the two women and the household were evacuated to next door. Later, after the fire was extinguished, Mr Lovell recovered the spent bomb that had caused his family so much inconvenience and kept it as a souvenir.

The house stills stands, close to the junction with Northwold Road at the southern end of the street. Alkham Road is a quiet, once well-to-do residential street of terraced houses. The nearest railway station is Stoke Newington, on the line to and from Liverpool Street station in the City of London.

See the entry for Balls Pond Road.

All Saints Church Cemetery, Harrow Weald

William Leefe Robinson VC, the first pilot to bring down an airship over British soil, was buried in All Saints Cemetery on 3 January 1919, after his death from influenza in nearby Stanmore. Hundreds of mourners turned out for the funeral procession, which was led by the Central Band of the RAF and saluted by a flight of aircraft.

Robinson's grave, which is tucked away in the corner entered from Elms Road, was subscribed by readers of the *Daily Express* and is in the form of a stone cross.

The grave of William Leefe Robinson VC, at Harrow Weald. Robinson shot down SL11 on 3 September 1916, the first German airship destroyed on British soil.

The base of the memorial states that it is:

> Sacred to the ever-loving memory of William Leefe Robinson VC, Captain Vth Battalion Worcestershire Regiment. Attached Royal Flying Corps. Born July 14th 1895 in South Coorg, India. Died December 31st 1891, at Harrow.

On the front of the grave is a quotation from Romans 4:17: 'God quickeneth the dead and calleth those which be not as though they were'. Along the side borders of the grave are the words:

> He was the first airman to attack a Zeppelin at night. After a most daring single handed fight he brought down L21 [SL11], a flaming wreck at Cuffley, on the 3rd September 1916. Thus, he led the way against the German Zeppelin peril threatening England.

And lines from Robert Browning's poem, *Epilogue:*

> One who never turn'd his back but marched breast forward,
> Never doubted clouds would break,
> Never dreamed, though right were worsted, wrong would triumph.
> Held we fall to rise, are baffled to fight better,
> Sleep to wake.

The grave is often visited and among the adorning flowers is a wreath sent each year by Robinson's old school of St Bee's in Cumbria. Visitors should note that the cemetery is along Uxbridge Road (A409), on the corner with Elms Road: it is not to be confused with the larger Harrow cemetery on the opposite (north) side of Uxbridge Road.

A minute's walk away from the grave, next to the larger cemetery, is a pub-restaurant named after the war hero, The William Leefe Robinson VC. On the walls of the bar are copies of letters and newspapers concerning Robinson, as well as souvenirs collected from SL11, including pieces of cable, melted metal and other fragments.

The graveyard and restaurant lie equidistant between the Harrow & Wealdstone and Stanmore Underground stations: regular buses that stop close to the site connect these. Harrow & Wealdstone is at the northernmost end of the Bakerloo Line by Tube; railway trains also serve the station. Stanmore is situated at the northernmost end of the Jubilee Line.

Balls Pond Road, Dalston

The three-storied house that stood at number 187 was hit during the first Zeppelin raid on London on the evening of 31 May 1915, killing two of the occupants, Henry and Caroline Good. Their deaths led to a public inquest, the details of which were widely reported and aroused strong emotions. The raider was *Hauptmann* Linnarz, in LZ38 who, minutes earlier, had dropped a bomb on 16 Alkham Road, and who was proceeding south over the Stoke Newington area.

The Goods occupied rooms at the back of the house on the second floor; across from them in a front room was Mrs Coningsby, an elderly widow; downstairs lived Mr T. Sharpling, the owner of the property, with his wife and children. When the house was bombed the Sharpling family rushed out into the garden where Mr Sharpling threw several bricks through the Goods' window to see if they were at home. There was no response, so it was assumed they were out. Meanwhile, at the front of the house Mrs Coningsby was forced to jump from the spreading flames into a blanket, after attempts to rescue her with too short ladders had proved unsuccessful.

Soon appearing on the scene was the Goods' son, Henry junior. He had heard the falling bombs and left his nearby home to check if his parents were all right. Forcing his way through gathering crowds, he found their building ablaze, but was assured by a fireman that everyone in the property had been taken out to safety. Fears grew for the couple as the hours lengthened, however. It was doubted whether they would possibly be out so late, but nothing could be confirmed until the morning when the fire had been brought under control. A policeman then put a ladder to the windows at the back of the house and climbed up. He saw the charred bodies of the couple kneeling by their bed, their clothes having been burnt off them. Mr Good's arm was clasped about his wife's waist. Because the bomb that had caused the tragedy exploded on the staircase and had caused no direct injury to the couple, the inquest found it difficult to ascertain the exact cause of death, but they were probably overcome by smoke before the flames engulfed them.

The site of the Goods' house has been built over several times since the early twentieth century; today it is occupied by a modern block of flats, on the corner of Southgate Road. Balls Pond Road lies on numerous bus routes; it is also situated between Canonbury and Dalston Kingsland railway stations.

See the entry for Alkham Road.

Bishopsgate Railway Goods Station, Shoreditch

Bishopsgate Railway Goods Station was an officially designated public air raid shelter. Nightly in 1917 and 1918 the local population, many of them foreign refugees, swarmed into the station regardless of whether there was a raid or not. They carried as many personal belongings, comforts, bedding and campstools as they possibly could, and conditions became so unsanitary after several months that the railway company barred access to the station until air raid warnings were actually sounded.

On the evening of 28 January 1918 hundreds were crowding the station gates, while across the road there was a large queue for the Olympia Music Hall performance. When warning maroons sounded they were mistaken for exploding bombs and those queuing joined the crowd already at the gates and rushed forward with them. Because the main gates were locked the mass of people stormed a smaller gateway, during which someone tripped trying to retrieve a campstool they had dropped. Men, women and children piled over each other. A mother had her baby knocked from her arms and trampled to death, others were crushed against the walls or suffocated. Fourteen lives were lost altogether, mostly women and children. The same night a similar stampede occurred at Mile End Underground Station in the East End, although, there, there were no fatalities.

The site of Bishopsgate Railway Goods Station is on the corner of Shoreditch High Street and Bethnal Green Road, a ten-minute walk northwards from Liverpool Street railway and Underground station. It now serves as a lorry and coach park after burning down in the 1960s. Liverpool Street station is served by the Central, Circle, Hammersmith & City and Metropolitan Lines.

Kenwood House, Highgate

From November 1915 to August 1916 Lieutenant Commander Rawlinson's RNAS Mobile Anti-Aircraft Brigade was based at Kenwood House. They were quartered in the Stable Block at the invitation of His Imperial Highness Grand Duke Michael Michaelovitch of Russia, the second cousin of the reigning Tsar, Nicholas II, who

The RNAS Mobile Anti-Aircraft Brigade on parade at Kenwood House, 5 December 1915. Imperial War Museum

A French 75mm Anti-Aircraft gun mounted on a De Dion Automobile chassis, being examined by Grand Duke Michael (looking at breech) and Admiral Percy Scott (beside him). Facing, in Army uniform but with Navy insignia, is Lieutenant Commander Alfred Rawlinson. Imperial War Museum

A 3-pounder Vickers gun on an AA mounting and Lancia chassis. Imperial War Museum

had leased Kenwood since 1910 (he was living in exile because of his morganatic marriage to Countess Torby). These barracks answered the Brigade's purposes admirably, as, with guns and men under one roof, they were constantly ready for action. In accordance with naval custom, the ratings slept in hammocks that were stowed away each morning; off duty they played cricket in the House's gardens or availed themselves of the golf course. Naturally enough, Rawlinson and his men enjoyed their time here. The Lieutenant Commander particularly relished joining the Grand Duke and his family for breakfast each morning, over which he would recollect the previous night's incidents – the splendour of the grand ducal table providing a welcome contrast to the slums of the East End where much of the Brigade's work was carried out. In August 1916 the Brigade moved to Norfolk.

Although there is no visible sign of Kenwood House's anti-aircraft role today, the Stable Block still stands and the place is worth visiting as a tourist attraction in its own right. Situated in a park beside Hampstead Heath, the House was remodelled by James and Robert Adam in the 1760s and 1770s, and is described by the architectural historian Nikolaus Pevsner as 'the finest eighteenth century country house in North London'. Since 1985 it has belonged to English Heritage and is open to the public with a fine collection of paintings.

Kenwood House is not located near any London Underground or railway stations, but buses run close by on Hampstead Lane.

Poplar Recreation Ground, Tower Hamlets

In the centre of the park stands a tall monument, erected by public subscription and surmounted by the statue of a grieving angel. Its inscription states that it was put up:

> *In memory of 18 children who were killed by a bomb dropped from a German aeroplane upon the L.C.C. School, Upper North Street, Poplar, on the 13th of June 1917.*

In raised lettering on the sides are listed the names and ages of the young victims of this incident – almost all of them five years old.

The leader of the German raiders that day, *Hauptmann* Brandenburg, had no idea that his men had bombed a school and caused this tragedy. He and the other bombers thought that they had successfully attacked a railway station, the Docks and Tower Bridge. It was fortunate that his England Squadron's poor accuracy had not resulted in worse catastrophe. Not far away from the Upper North Street elementary school

The memorial to the children killed by a bomb on their school in Poplar, 13 June 1917.

107

there was a lucky escape for pupils at the Cowper Street Foundation School in City Road, where a bomb similar to the one that fell on the school in Poplar penetrated five floors but failed to detonate.

Poplar Recreation Ground is on East India Dock Road, close to both Poplar and All Saints stations on the Docklands Light Railway. Upper North Street runs north from East India Road, roughly 250 yards west of the recreation ground.

Royal Air Force Museum, Hendon

During the First World War Hendon was an important aeroplane manufacturing area, producing De Havillands and Blériot Experimentals, and home to an airfield. Based here in September 1915 were two of the four RNAS BE2cs – the others were at Chingford in north-east London – that were the only aircraft guarding London; from February to May 1916 the RFC had two BE2cs here; after this Hendon was used as a training base by the RFC School of Instruction, 18 Wing. Although the airfield has long since been built over and the aeroplane factories have disappeared, the brick and wooden structure of two aircraft hangars dating from 1917 remain. These listed buildings have been incorporated into the Main Aircraft Hall of the Royal Air Force Museum.

Some of the most interesting material is to be found in Bomber Hall. Here there is a DH9a day bomber, No. F1010, which was based at Bettencourt in France and was used to bomb Kaiserslautern. It was brought down on 5 October 1918 and taken to Berlin as a trophy for the Air Museum there. Nearby there is a replica of Sopwith Tabloid No. 168, as flown by Flight Lieutenant Reginald Marix on 8 October 1914, when he successfully bombed the German Army airship shed at Düsseldorf, destroying ZIX. Next to this Tabloid is a replica Vickers Vimy, a long-range bomber developed for the bombing of Germany and capable of delivering a bomb load of 4,804lb, but which entered service in 1919, too late to be used in the war. Also in this hall are several examples of British bombs, including a 1,650lb bomb – the largest type used by the British – intended for use against industry in the German town of Essen.

In the Upper Floor Galleries are displayed the medals of Captain G. W. Murlis Green; he was awarded a second bar to his Military Cross for his success on 18 December 1917 when he became the first pilot to shoot down a Gotha during a night raid. In a room celebrating airmen decorated with VCs, Warneford and Robinson are remembered, and accompanying Robinson's display is a silver cigarette case presented by him to Sowrey, and a wooden ashtray crafted from one of SL11's propeller blades. In a gallery devoted to First World War aviation German Army and Navy badges are exhibited; they include a Commemorative Army Airship Crew Badge.

In the Main Aircraft Hall are a variety of First World War aeroplanes. As well as a RFC training aeroplane, there are numerous fighter aircraft, including a Bristol F2b Fighter (uncovered along one side to reveal its structure), a Sopwith Pup, a Sopwith Triplane, a Sopwith Camel, an SE5a, a Belgian Hanriot HD4 and a German Fokker DVII. The exterior of the forward control car of the British airship R33, built in 1919 and closely based on the design of the German L33 that came down in Essex, may be seen protruding from an upper wall. It backs on to the Upper Floor Galleries from where the car's interior may be examined.

The nearest Underground station to the Museum is Colindale, on the Northern Line, from where it is signposted.

Warrington Crescent where Giant R39 dropped a 1,000kg (2,200lb) during the raid of 7/8 March 1918. Such was the destruction and loss of life that members of the royal family made personal visits to the scene. Here, in the middle distance, Lord French, the Commander-in-Chief of Home Forces, escorts the King and Queen. Imperial War Museum

Warrington Crescent, Maida Vale

It was in this quiet suburban street that the leader of the Giant Squadron, *Hauptmann* von Bentivegni aboard R39, dropped one of his 1,000kg (2,200lb) explosives during a raid carried out on the night of 7/8 March 1918. The bomb fell just after midnight on the Friday morning, crashing on top of the dividing wall between numbers 63 and 65 on the western side of the Crescent. Both apartment buildings, those adjoining either side of them and one on the opposite side of the road were demolished by the tremendous blast; another 140 houses were affected, twenty of them within a seventy yard radius being seriously damaged. According to an eyewitness:

> *The four houses were reduced to hideous piles of wreckage. Across the road great branches of plane trees were torn from the stem, massive iron railings were thrown down and smashed, paving stones were torn up, and the contents of half a dozen houses were tossed about in a broken and tangled litter.... For a couple of hundred yards in every direction hardly a window, even in basement rooms, was left intact.*

Of the residents of the street, twelve were killed and twenty-three injured. The scale of the destruction was such that Queen Alexandra and Princess Victoria came to visit the stricken area next afternoon, the King and Queen making a personal inspection on the Saturday.

Forty-two Home Defence aeroplanes attempted to intercept von Bentivegni and the four other Giants that raided that night, but none succeeded because of the cloudy weather; indeed, the poor conditions caused the death of two RFC pilots, Captain Alexander Kynoch flying a BE12 and Captain Henry Stroud in a SE5a. They collided in midair near Shotgate in Essex. (See the entry for Shotgate, Essex.) The only evidence of the devastation in Warrington Crescent today is the large gap in the original Victorian terrace where numbers 61-67 once stood. The ruins were only partially filled in after 1918 with a low row of two-storey, mock-Tudor houses.

The nearest Tube station is Warwick Avenue on the Bakerloo Line.

Woolwich Arsenal, Woolwich

The importance of the Royal Arsenal at Woolwich as a munitions factory made it the objective of many air raids during the Great War and it was lucky to escape severe damage. However, *Kapitänleutnant* Mathy, commanding L13, managed to strike the Arsenal with a 300kg (660lb) bomb near midnight on 13/14 October 1915. The large explosion killed nine men within the Arsenal itself and another four in Woolwich Barracks. A Giant inflicted further casualties later on in the war, but this was by accident. When R12 under *Oberleutnant* Hans-Joachim von Seydlitz-Gerstenberg collided with the balloon apron over Woolwich on 16/17 February 1918 two of his 300kg bombs were pulled from their racks. Falling on the Arsenal, they killed two men in the barracks and five in Artillery Place; another two were wounded and the garrison chapel was damaged.

Recently, Woolwich Arsenal has undergone redevelopment and part has opened as Firepower, the Royal Artillery Museum. This devotes considerable space to the artillery of the First World War and in the Gunnery Hall there is a Mark III 3-inch Anti-Aircraft gun dating from 1918. This type was the first British artillery piece designed exclusively for anti-aircraft use. It was mounted on a lorry or a pedestal and its shells could reach 23,400ft. An interactive video is alongside the piece.

Trains run direct to Woolwich Arsenal from Charing Cross, London Bridge and Cannon Street railway stations.

ENGLAND

(excluding London)

CAMBRIDGESHIRE

Imperial War Museum, Duxford

An airfield was begun here in 1917 and was used as an assembly point for DH9 day bombers en route to France. Duxford ended the war as a training depot. From that time there remain Hangars 3, 4 and 5, which were built in 1917; these listed buildings retain their original wooden roofs. Contemporary with them is the Temporary Exhibition Gallery, which was a carpenters' workshop.

Although the focus at Duxford is on the Second World War and the Battle of Britain, there are several superb items relating to the First World War air raids and defence. In Hangar 4 visitors may see a Bristol F2B Fighter, a fast and manoeuvrable two-seater. This one, No. E2581, was issued to No. 39 Home Defence Squadron at North Weald in September 1918. Alongside this aeroplane is a RFC mobile workshop replete with power tools, lathes, drills and hand tools. These workshops were mounted on 3-ton Leyland lorries because the RFC lacked permanent buildings and facilities for much of the war, their mobility proving useful when it was necessary to recover aeroplanes that crash-landed away from the airfield. Next to this is a Thornycroft J-Type lorry with a 13-pounder AA gun fitted on the chassis, from 1916. Also in the hangar is an example of a German Maybach aero engine, as fitted in Zeppelins and Giants. All these exhibits have been restored to mint condition. In Hangar 1 there is a 100kg (220lb) German bomb, the tail fins of which were angled to spin-stabilize it during its descent and activate the fuses by centrifugal force. The fact that these fins are intact suggests this particular bomb was never dropped – they were usually ripped off on impact with the ground.

In the Land Warfare Hall are displayed First World War army limbers, wagons and German and British field guns.

DERBYSHIRE

Derby

Warnings were sounded in Derby early in the evening of 31 January 1916, when a number of Zeppelins targeted the Midlands. The city was left untouched as the raiders went westwards, one of them, *Kapitänleutnant der Reserve* Böcker in L14, flying over Nottingham and Derby on his way to attack Liverpool. Thick cloud hindered him in his objective, however, and after a couple of hours he returned east to drop bombs in the south of the county near Overseal and Swadlincote. By this time many in Derby thought the danger of several hours earlier was over and, as a consequence, the Special Constables had gone home and lighting restrictions had eased. Thus, when Böcker re-arrived at Derby – whose lights he mistook for the factories and blast furnaces of nearby Nottingham – no one was prepared for the bombs that began dropping at 12.07 am.

The first of a series of high explosives exploded in the Midland Railway maintenance works, killing three workmen there (William Bancroft, James Hardy and Harry Hithersay) and injuring two more, one of whom died soon afterwards (Charles Champion). More bombs wrought material damage to the Metalite Lamp Works in Gresham Street, and an incendiary in Horton Street caused a small fire. Two explosives on Derby Gas Company rendered no harm, though, and other devices released by L14 were also inoffensive, landing on unoccupied land or failing to detonate. However, a retired headmistress, Sarah Constantine, died as a result of heart failure brought on by the raid.

Although Derby Museum and Art Gallery, on The Strand, has no items connected with this raid, the Museum does have among its exhibits a small box containing fragments of the naval Zeppelin shot down at Theberton in June 1917 – *Kapitänleutnant der Reserve* Franz Eichler's L48. (See the entry for Theberton, Suffolk.)

See the entries for Birmingham and Walsall in the West Midlands, Loughborough in Leicestershire and Burton upon Trent in Staffordshire.

Ilkeston

On the evening of 31 January 1916 L20, commanded by *Kapitänleutnant* Franz Stabbert, raided Ilkeston after an earlier attack on Loughborough in Leicestershire. The Stanton Iron Works were hit with fifteen bombs, killing two and wounding two. Stabbert then went on to Burton upon Trent for his main action that night.

DURHAM

Annfield Plain

Along West Road stands an obelisk dedicated to the memory of Sergeant Arthur John Joyce, No. 36 Squadron, RFC, who crashed and died here after taking off from Hylton airbase in a FE2b on the evening of 13 March 1918. He was on defensive patrol during the Zeppelin raid in which Hartlepool was attacked by L42

The memorial to Sergeant Arthur Joyce, who crashed his FE2b at Annfield Plain while making a defensive sortie, 13 March 1918.
Imperial War Museum

A close-up of the inscription.

IT WAS HERE SERGᵀ PILOT JOYCE MET HIS DEATH ON THE NIGHT OF MARCH 13ᵀᴴ 1918

(*Kapitänleutnant* Martin Dietrich). He flew into the hill of Pontop Pike, either by accident or as a forced landing, just before 11.00 pm.

The monument was erected by the inhabitants of Annfield Plain and district in 1919 and rededicated fifty years later by the Stanley Branch of the Royal Air Forces Association. It records Sergeant Joyce's own words: 'Our lives are not our own, they belong to our Country'. The bottom stone details his son, Sergeant Observer Dennis Arthur Joyce, who went missing believed killed in September 1940 while flying over Germany.

Hartlepool

On the night of 27/28 November 1916 the German Navy's L34 attacked Hartlepool and was brought down in the sea. Commanded by *Kapitänleutnant der Reserve* Max Dietrich, the Zeppelin had been caught by the Castle Eden searchlight at 11.30 pm and seen by Second Lieutenant Ian V. Pyott in a BE2c. He dived beneath and shot at the Zeppelin, then pursued it as the airship continued towards the town at a speed of 70mph. Dietrich released bombs over West Hartlepool in order to gain height and safety and swung seaward, but Pyott had time to direct long bursts into the Zeppelin's left side. Flames appeared and quickly spread. Seen seventy miles away to the south by L22, one of the crew, *Oberleutnant zur See* Richard Frey, observed L34's end:

> The heat of the burning gas made the entire framework red hot, and this outlined the form of the ship sharply against the dark sky. The fall seemed to last several minutes and we saw her break into two pieces on the sea.

The Zeppelin fell a mile offshore of the River Tees; all on board died. The explosives that it had dropped killed four and injured eleven, the worst of the bomb damage befalling Hartley Street, Lowthian Road, Poplar Grove and Rugby Terrace in West Hartlepool. *Kapitänleutnant* Herbert Ehrlich in L35, ten miles to the north, might have followed up the assault, but the sight of Dietrich's destruction prompted him to forsake his raid.

On the night of 13/14 March 1918 Max Dietrich's namesake, *Kapitänleutnant* Martin Dietrich, avenged the formers' loss with another attack on Hartlepool. On board L42, he ignored Strasser's orders to return home after strong winds were forecast and waited off the English coast till night fell. Having intercepted the wireless recall, British defences were not on alert. Hartlepool was not warned of a possible raid and its bright lights presented an easy target to the incoming Zeppelin. Bombs were dropped from 16,400ft, the majority again on West Hartlepool, where Temperance Street, Frederick Street, Whitby Street and Burbank Street were hit. Of the eight that were killed, an old man, two children and a baby perished in the same house at 23 Temperance Street. Another twenty-nine persons were injured. Dietrich returned to Nordholz expecting to be reprimanded by Strasser for his disobedience – instead the Leader of Airships styled him 'Count of Hartlepool' in honour of the raid.

At the Museum of Hartlepool, Hartlepool Marina, there is a small display about the so-called 'Count of Hartlepool' and the shooting down of L34, along with pieces of the fallen Zeppelin.

Kapitänleutnant *Martin Dietrich, commander of L42, nicknamed the 'Count of Hartlepool' after his raid on that city, 13 March 1918.* Imperial War Museum

Evenwood

Oberleutnant zur See Peterson blew up fifteen cottages and damaged many more here, early on 5/6 April 1916; a man and a child lost their lives. The Zeppelin, L16, targeted collieries on its way back out to sea, killing four more in the area.

EAST RIDING OF YORKSHIRE

Goole

In the late evening of 9 August 1915 *Kapitänleutnant* Loewe, with L9, approached the Humber Estuary. He waited off the coast until it was completely dark then came inland at 11.15 pm to raid Hull. Ground mist obscured the boundary between sea and shore, however, and, combined with a rudder defect that obliged his Zeppelin to go around in circles before it could be repaired, Loewe lost his way. When he eventually located what he thought was his objective, he was actually twenty miles away to the east over Goole. Although this town's lights had been shaded to avoid discovery, their reflection on the damp pavements below could just be made out from on board the airship. Loewe's bombs claimed sixteen lives, demolished ten houses and damaged warehouses in the town. Thinking his mission against Hull's docks had been accomplished, the commander withdrew and claimed to have come under heavy anti-aircraft fire.

Hull

As a large city and port on the eastern coast of England, it was guaranteed that Hull would be attacked by German airships. In the course of the conflict the city endured no less than fifty-three warnings, or 'buzzers' as they were known locally. Hull experienced its first air raid on 6/7 June 1915 when naval Zeppelin L9, under *Kapitänleutnant* Mathy, approached from the direction of Bridlington. Thick ground mist veiled the Yorkshire countryside and it took a couple of hours before the commander located his quarry at midnight. He then used parachute flares to illuminate the port and dropped thirteen high explosives and dozens of incendiaries. Mathy felt certain he had set the docks ablaze and blown up a gas works, but what he had mostly hit were working class terraces and business premises. The worst hit streets were Campbell Street, South Parade, Edwin's Place, East Street, Waller Street, Queen Street and Market Place, where the Edwin Davis & Co. grand department store was reduced to rubble, along with all its contents. The large fire that lit up the town and sky for miles around was not the gas works but a timber yard. Of the dead, nineteen were buried under debris or burned in their beds; another five died of shock without having being touched by the bombs. The only resistance offered against the raider came from the 4-inch guns of HMS *Adventure*, a small cruiser that was under repair in the port.

Hull was no better defended when the second major raid occurred on 5/6 March 1916. This time two Zeppelins ravaged the city. First to arrive was *Kapitänleutnant der Reserve* Böcker in L14, blown south after trying for the Tyne. At midnight he dropped six bombs in fields near Beverley before flying over Hull at 9,500ft and releasing seven explosives and thirteen incendiaries, which mainly fell on houses by the docks. Winds prevented Böcker making a second bomb run and his airship

A Hull couple inspect damage caused to their property on the night of 6/7 June 1915. It was Hull's first air raid, carried out by **Kapitänleutnant** *Mathy in L9.* Hull Museums

limped home with water contaminating and freezing the engines and St Elmo's Fire breaking out on board. Ten minutes after L14's departure at 1.00 am came L11, under *Korvettenkapitän* Schütze. He had been hoping to reach Middlesbrough, but headwinds held him in check until he too was forced to seek an alternative target. After locating Flamborough Head, Hull stood out to the south as a dark patch on the snowy landscape and L14's bombs could be seen exploding. When he reached Hull, Schütze descended to 4,000ft and hovered steadily over the city for twenty minutes. Over one and a half tons of bombs rained down, damaging a steamer in Earle's dry dock, blowing up houses and sheds, and setting fire to the Mariners' Almshouses. Linnaeus Street, Queen Street (again), Regent Street, High Street and Colliers Street were the most affected areas. Schütze flew away south, dropping four bombs on Killingholme on the other side of the Humber before heading out to sea. The combined death toll attributable to the two Zeppelins was eighteen and over fifty citizens were wounded. Indignation about the Zeppelins' ability to raid at will for an hour caused a military transport vehicle to be attacked in Hull, while in Beverley, where no one had been hurt, a RFC officer was molested. Among the examples of grim humour was the suggestion that the next time they came 'the Germans would put down a ladder and get out'. At least, though, the city was promised genuine anti-aircraft guns to supplement its dummy wooden one on top of a works roof. And to make sure they were not duped a second time, a committee of citizens was formed to inspect the batteries regularly.

When Schütze and L11 returned to Hull a month later, on 5 April, the commander found its defences vastly improved. AA forced the Zeppelin to retire without dropping a bomb on the city, but still a woman died of fright. On 8/9 August, however, *Kapitänleutnant* Robert Koch in L24 dropped forty bombs to cause ten dead and twenty injured – the anti-aircraft batteries this time hampered by poor visibility. The penultimate attack on Hull was by *Hauptman* Kuno Manger's L41 at 2.40 am on 25 September 1917, but with little harm. Finally, *Kapitänleutnant* von Freudenreich dropped a dozen bombs from L63 in the early hours of 13 March 1918: these fell on the northern reaches of Hull and surrounding countryside, and aside from a cow at Cottingham, the only death was, as the *Hull Times* would later describe, 'a result of shock through fear of air raids'.

Kilnsea

Close to the village of Kilnsea there is a surviving example of a sound mirror, a primitive early warning device developed in the Great War by the Munitions Inventions Department to detect approaching raiders on the east coast. These concrete, shallow concave devices amplified the thrum of engines from a distance and, although fixed, could pick up sound waves from different directions. A listener in front of the mirror used a trumpet-shaped sound collector and stethoscope to focus the reverberations and, as the collector was attached to a system of quadrant pointers, by moving this over the surface of the mirror the listener was able to plot the bearing and altitude of approaching craft. Electrical microphones were adopted later in the war to aid listeners, and experimentation with sound mirrors continued in the post-war period, until the development of radar rendered them obsolete.

The 15ft diameter sound mirror at Kilnsea is probably of a later type than those found at Boulby, Redcar and Sunderland and is differently shaped, with no projecting sides. Uniquely, the metal post survives on which the reception device was mounted in front of the convex surface.

The sound mirror at Kilnsea. A number of these concrete structures were built along the east coast to detect approaching enemy aircraft.

The structure is located in a field slightly north of Grange Farm, on land belonging to the neighbouring farmer. No public right of way exists, but good views of the sound mirror may be obtained from the road to Kilnsea, as well as from the seaward side (for the latter, drive through the village and park near the seaside caravan site, then walk along the private road to the dunes).

For other sound mirrors see the entries for Boulby and Redcar in North Yorkshire, and Sunderland, Tyne & Wear.

ESSEX

Colchester

Colchester was attacked at 8.45 pm on 21 February 1915 by a lone raider, *Oberleutnant zur See* Stephan von Prondzynski, flying a Friedrichshafen FF29 seaplane, with *Fähnrich zur See* Heym as his observer. They attacked Butt Road, near the town centre, and damaged buildings at Colchester barracks. Earlier in the evening they had released two incendiary devices at Braintree and a bomb outside Coggeshall. On their return journey the Germans developed engine trouble and alighted off the coast; they were picked up and taken prisoner a couple of days later. Photographs and postcards relating to the Colchester raid are held at Hollytrees Museum, next to Castle Park. The Museum also has aluminium struts from L33 and other ephemera concerning the First World War air raids, but usually only displays a silver watch that was awarded to Alfred Wright by the Essex Police Constabulary, for his efforts in the early hours of 24 September 1916 when L33 came down at Little Wigborough. He was injured in a car crash while summoning help and died a couple of months afterwards.

See the entry for Little Wigborough, where Wright is buried in St Nicholas's churchyard.

Great Burstead, near Billericay

L32, commanded by *Oberleutnant zur See* Peterson, was shot down by Second Lieutenant Frederick Sowrey on the night of 23/24 September 1916. It was a clear night and the flaming Zeppelin was visible for many miles around as it slowly descended, coming down at Snails Hall Farm on the corner of Outwood Road and Green Farms Lane in Great Burstead at 1.20 am. Although not the first German airship to have been brought down, tens of thousands were eager to see the doomed craft, or what was left of it, in the next few days. Trains from Liverpool Street Station were packed and the roads were jammed with cars, bicycles and pedestrians, all slowly inching their way to the site, a mile and a half south of Billericay. The tangled wreckage of the Zeppelin looked to one journalist like the skeleton of a monstrous dinosaur. While soldiers with fixed bayonets stood guard and RFC officers sorted through the remains, members of the public scoured nearby fields for pieces as souvenirs. The twenty-two dead crew members had been placed out of sight in a barn – all were burnt beyond recognition except for Peterson.

The crew were buried in the churchyard of Great Burstead with full military honours several days later, watched by a handful of people. Unlike at Potters Bar a few weeks earlier, the service was dignified and uninterrupted by protests, though

Gondola and wreckage of naval Zeppelin L32 at Snails Hall Farm, Great Burstead. Shot down by Second Lieutenant Sowrey with the loss of all hands on 24 September 1916. Imperial War Museum

Parts of L32 on show to the public, including framework, bomb switchboard and the commander Oberleutnant zur See *Peterson's chair.* Imperial War Museum

critics afterwards railed against the honour accorded the 'baby killers and murderers'.

A number of L32 items are on display at the Cater Museum in Billericay High Street, including souvenirs made from the framework and a flare canister. Photographs and postcards complement a display about the Zeppelin raids and there is even a miniature model reconstruction of L32's dying moments. Booklets regarding the airship are also on sale. Elsewhere in the Museum, tucked away in one of the glass cabinets filled with old household ephemera, is a charming tiny monument in the form of a cross and aeroplane made from part of the Gotha which came down at Rochford on 6 December 1917.

For more about this Gotha see the entry for Rochford in Essex.

Little Wigborough

L33 came down gently in a field between Little Wigborough and Peldon not long after 1.00 am on 24 September 1916. Commanded by *Kapitänleutnant der Reserve* Böcker, the Zeppelin had been returning from a raid on London when it was damaged by anti-aircraft fire. Losing hydrogen and height, L33 was unable to make it home and turned back from the North Sea to ditch on dry land. Böcker tried to warn the inhabitants of the cottages next to where his airship lay that he would fire the craft, but one family, the Routs, refused to answer the door and hid inside a cupboard. As it was, there was too little gas left in the Zeppelin to burn more than the envelope and to singe the fur of a white terrier dog that was sniffing around. Böcker then marched his men up the road towards Peldon where Special Constable Edgar Nicholas met them on his bicycle. He asked if they were German and if they were surrendering, to which they replied yes, and he marched them quietly away to

Lloyd George, along with other dignitaries, inspecting the wreckage of L33.
Imperial War Museum

The grave of Alfred Wright who was fatally injured the night L33 crash-landed at Little Wigborough.

captivity. The fate of these uninjured crewmen could have been much worse. Earlier, above Chelmsford, they were fortunate that Second Lieutenant Brandon had not destroyed them in flames: when he attacked, the Zeppelin had been unable to defend itself after jettisoning most of its machine guns to gain altitude. Brandon, whose bullets were afterwards found to have peppered the airship's petrol tanks, had been similarly unsuccessful in April when attacking L15 (see the entry for Margate).

The recovered structure of L33 was subsequently copied by Britain and used to design its post-war airships R33 and R34; in 1919 the latter was the first airship to cross the Atlantic. On a more intimate note, the airship inspired the choice of name for a baby girl born to the Clark family in Great Wigborough the day it came down: she was christened Zeppelina.

In the centre of St Nicholas's churchyard, at the end of Copt Lane, is the grave of Alfred Wright, a forty-five-year-old seed grower from the village. He left home on his motorcycle to summon assistance when the Zeppelin landed, but he crashed with a car and shattered one of his legs. He died in hospital from his injuries nearly two months later, on 13 November. A path had to be cut through L33's wreckage to allow the funeral cortège through to the church. Inside St Nicholas's there is a girder piece of the airship and an explanatory plaque.

See the entry for Colchester: the silver watch awarded to Alfred Wright by the Essex Police Constabulary is displayed there at the Hollytrees Museum.

North Weald Bassett

An important airbase in two world wars, the RFC airfield at North Weald was begun in 1916. In July or August that year A Flight of No. 39 Squadron moved in here with eleven aeroplanes as part of the programme of stiffening London's air defences. The men were billeted in tents and the officers in local houses. A 13-pounder gun and a searchlight protected the site. During the 1917 Gotha offensive B and C Flights joined North Weald from Hainault Farm and Suttons Farm to form a complete squadron. In May 1918 Bristol F2Bs of No. 75 Squadron moved here before being sent to France for the last few weeks of war.

Famous pilots based here during the war include Second Lieutenant Wulstan Tempest. He set off at 10.00 pm on the night of 1 October 1916 in a BE2c, armed, contrary to regulations, with only a single Lewis gun and a reduced amount of ammunition. So lightened, he overcame Mathy aboard L31 at Potters Bar a couple of hours later. Returning to North Weald, Tempest dizzily miscalculated his altitude and crash-landed, but survived. Other notables were Lieutenant Anthony Arkell and First Air Mechanic Albert Stagg. In Arkell's Bristol Fighter, 'Devil in the Dusk', they brought down a Gotha in the East End of London during the England Squadron's ultimate raid on England, on the night of Whitsunday, 19 May 1918. *Vizefeldwebel* Hans Thiedke and Paul Sapkowiak (rank unknown) leapt to their deaths from the stricken plane; *Gefreiter* Wilhelm Schulte perished in the crash.

Lieutenant Arkell (right) and First Air Mechanic Stagg (left), inspecting the wreckage of the Gotha which they shot down in East London in the early hours of 20 May 1918. Although they fired hundreds of rounds of bullets between them at the Gotha, it was Stagg who got in the decisive shot. Interestingly, it was Stagg's first time in Arkell's Bristol Fighter. They were based at North Weald. Imperial War Museum

Of the First World War base today only the staff building on Hurricane Way remains, Ad Astra House. This hosts the voluntarily run North Weald Airfield Museum and is close to the original main entrance of the airfield. Although the majority of material on display relates to the Second World War, more space and attention will be devoted to the RFC and early RAF period in future. In front of Ad Astra House is a granite stone memorial honouring those who died while stationed at North Weald – more than 250 airmen in the two world wars.

Rochford

After serving as a RFC night flying training station with No. 37 Squadron, on 2 August 1917 Rochford also became the home of No. 61 Squadron. This was at first equipped with Sopwith Pups, then SE5as, and later Sopwith Camels. In June 1918 No. 152 Squadron was established here with Camel night fighters and No. 37 left the aerodrome; No. 152 transferred to France in October.

Of the many aeroplanes to have visited Rochford during the First World War perhaps the most remarkable was a Gotha, which crash-landed here at 4.45 am on 6 December 1917. It had been damaged by AA near Canvey Island and was losing height when it saw the flares of the aerodrome to the north-east. The Gotha decided to head for these and, as it neared, fired a Very light. Captain Cecil Lewis (who had been transferred to No. 61 Squadron) recalled what happened next in his memoirs, *Sagittarius Rising*:

> We had three colours of lights – red, green, and white. The colour was changed daily, a sort of password. The Gotha, heaven knows how, fired the right colour, was answered from the ground, and came in to land. Unfortunately, not knowing the aerodrome, the pilot miscalculated, hit a tree on the edge of it, and slewed round, crashing on to the golf-course. The mechanics rushed down, thinking it was one of our machines, and found the Hun crew of three, one officer and two N.C.Os., climbing out of the wreckage. They were taken prisoners. All were quite unhurt. Some officers turned out to inspect the wreckage and remove the bombs, of which there were two hundred-pounders and about twenty babies. They also took out the Very Light pistol and the cartridges. The machine was pretty well smashed up and the tanks had burst, flooding the ground with petrol. The Equipment Officer, who had taken the Very Light pistol, slipped it into the pocket of his mackintosh. As he walked away, he pulled it out to show to one of the others. The trigger had no guard, caught in his pocket flap, and the pistol went off. The white-hot magnesium flare bounced along the ground, reached the petrol, and instantly the whole wreckage was in flames. Next morning, only the charred iron-work of the fuselage, the engines and wires were left. We were very upset about this, because, at that time, a great controversy raged as to whether the rear gunner in the Gotha had a tunnel to enable him to fire under his tail.

The Gotha's crew were *Leutnant* R Wessells (commander-navigator), *Vizefeldwebel* O. Jacobs (gunner) and *Gemeiner* J. Rzechtalski (pilot).

In the village of Rochford several RFC and RAF airmen are buried in the parish churchyard of St Andrew's, among them Captain Stroud who was killed on patrol on 7 March 1918 when his SE5a collided with another Home Defence plane, from No. 37 Squadron, Stow Maries. Inside the church, on the left of nave, there is a marble memorial 'In Proud and Loving Memory' of the twenty-four-year-old. Near it is a propeller-cross with a plaque to Lieutenant John Wilton Sheridan, also of No. 61 Squadron, who died on 27 September 1918. He is one of those buried beside Captain Stroud.

For a fuller account of Stroud's fatal accident see the following entry for Shotgate. For the story of another Gotha that came down on 6 December 1917 see the entry for Canterbury in Kent.

Shotgate

In the fields of Dollyman's Farm are two railed-off monuments in remembrance of RFC pilots Captain Kynoch, No. 37 Squadron, and Captain Stroud, No. 61 Squadron. They flew into each other on the night of 7/8 March 1918 when London was raided by Giants. Kynoch, in a BE12, and Stroud, in a SE5a, probably hit each other while climbing through cloud over Rayleigh. Their aeroplanes fell in adjacent fields and Kynoch's body was recovered some distance from his machine.

Both monuments marking where they fell are neglected and overgrown. The metal lettering on Kynoch's, near the railway embankment, is barely readable but states:

> Sacred to the Memory of Capt. Alexander Bruce Kynoch, RAF, who was killed in action here on the night of March 7th 1918. Aged 24 Years.

Stroud's memorial is a couple of hundred yards away. In front of a metal propeller on a rusty column a stone bears the words:

> This spot is sacred to the memory of Capt. Henry Clifford Stroud, NCR and RFC. Killed in action at midnight 7th March 1918. Faithful unto death.

Dollyman's Farm is on the south side of the A129, halfway between Wickford and Rayleigh.

Wickford itself is where the first Gotha shot down on land by British aeroplanes fell at 10.10 pm on 28 January 1918. The pilots responsible were No. 44 Squadron's Captain George Hackwill and Second Lieutenant Charles Banks, both in Sopwith Camels. They closed on the bomber at 10,000ft, Banks to the left, Hackwill to the right, making it difficult for the German gunner to bear on them. They strafed the Gotha for ten minutes before flames appeared and it plunged earthwards, blowing up on impact in a field at Frund's Farm. The crew of the Gotha were *Leutnant* Friedrich von Thomsen, navigator and commander, and his two *Unteroffiziers*, gunner Walter Heiden and pilot Karl Ziegler; all three lost their lives.

See the entry for Rochford: Captain Stroud is buried there at St Andrew's Church.

The dilapidated memorial to Captain Alexander Kynoch, marking where he crashed, near Shotgate, after a midair collision with another British pilot, Captain Henry Stroud. They were flying in defence of London on the night of 7/8 March 1918.

Southend-on-Sea

When Southend was raided in the early hours of 10 May 1915, 'and the war, which to most of us is only an abstract thing, came to our very doors', eyewitnesses claimed to have seen up to four different airships. In fact, only one craft was responsible: Army Zeppelin LZ38, commanded by *Hauptmann* Linnarz. Starting at 2.45 am, the airship flew east to west and back 'shedding bombs like peas'. More than a hundred were dropped on the coastal town and its neighbours, over half of them falling in the centre of Southend and the Prittlewell and Westcliff areas. The list of locations where damage occurred included Ashburnham Road, York Road East, Ambleside Drive, Victoria Avenue, Richmond Avenue, Baxter Avenue, Toledo Road, Royal Terrace, Prittlewell Square, Essex Street, Scratton Road, St Vincent's Road, St John's Road, Coleman Street, Clifton Mews, Grange Gardens, Princes Street, behind London Road, the back of Cambridge Road, Tudor Road, Westborough School playground, West Road and the rear of Harcourt Avenue. Several houses were set ablaze and Flaxman's timber yard in Southchurch Road was burnt out.

Occupants of the Cromwell boarding house in London Road had a narrow escape. When Mrs Samme, the landlady, went to her daughter's room to wake her an incendiary pierced the roof and passed within feet of them as it continued on through the floor and into the front room below, where it finally exploded. The Sammes and their guests fled into the street half-naked as the place was gutted. Less fortunate was the resident of 120 North Road, where another incendiary device fell. An elderly lady, Mrs Agnes Frances Whitwell, burnt to death there.

A steam whistle installed at the electricity station blew minutes after the raid was over; its only effect was to draw outside those who were not already sightseeing in their slippers. The *Southend Standard*, which angered the government by publishing a detailed supplement about the raid a week later, reported:

> *The authorities' warning to remain quietly indoors was as if it had never been given. We Britishers are not going to sit mum at home whenever there is a sight to be seen out of mere consideration of safety; so Southend in its thousands crowded the streets.*

The numbers were swelled the next day by an influx of Londoners.

One bomb, recovered from the garden of 11 Rayleigh Avenue, had a piece of cardboard attached with the message in blue pencil: 'You English. We have come + we'll come again soon. Kill or cure. German.' True to their words, Linnarz and LZ38 returned a week later and raided Margate, and then on 26 May at 11.15 pm bombed Southend for a second time. Its seventy bombs on this occasion killed three and wounded three.

The worst raid that the resort experienced came on Sunday, 12 August 1917 at the hands of twelve Gothas. Deterred by AA from an attack on Chatham, these approached Southend via Leigh-on-Sea just before 6.00 pm. Bombs dropped along the coastal strip damaged over thirty houses and claimed over thirty lives. Most of the casualties occurred when a salvo of 50kg (110lb) devices, presumably aimed at the Great Eastern Railway station, blew up in Victoria Avenue which was thronged with churchgoers and holidaymakers. Fifteen lives were lost here; the total was brought up by further 50kg bombs in Milton Street and Guildford Road.

No alarm was raised and the nearby anti-aircraft batteries remained silent during the attack, but it could have been worse. Only half of the bombs dropped by the Germans went off.

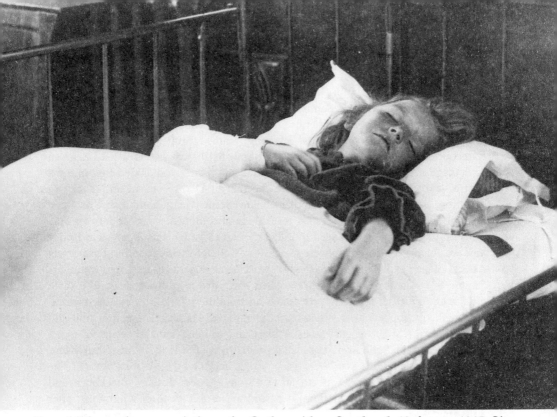

Two children who were victims of a Gotha raid on Southend, 12 August 1917. Six-year-old Constance Betty, injured in her arms and legs, and Tommy Grant, also hurt in the arms and legs, who lost a brother in the attack. Imperial War Museum

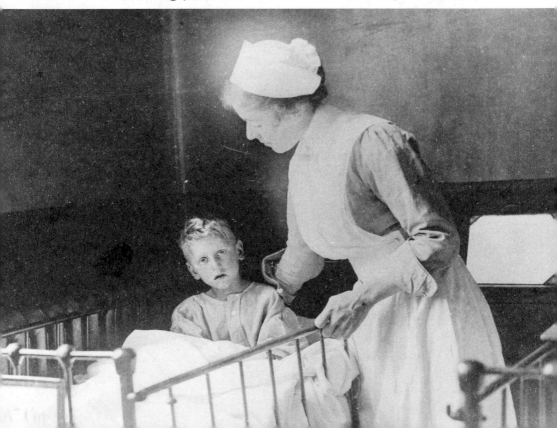

GREATER MANCHESTER

Bolton

Bolton was raided on 26 September 1916 by L21, under the command of *Oberleutnant zur See* Frankenberg. The Zeppelin, which had already bombed Rawtenstall and Holcombe that evening, came from the north-east over Ramsbottom then Astley Bridge where a bomb fell harmlessly in a field near an orphanage at 12.20 am. The airship proceeded south-west and circled Bolton town centre – which Frankenberg believed to be that of Derby – in an anti-clockwise direction, clearly visible to the onlookers below. Some twenty bombs were dropped in total and, although several failed to explode and the gas works and Town Hall were missed, the raider managed to inflict considerable damage. A house in Lodge Vale was blown up, two more were wrecked in Wellington Street and in Kirk Street a series of high explosives demolished six working class cottages in a row – numbers 58, 60, 62, 64 and 66. Thirteen were killed here (five men, five women and three girls) while a further fourteen were recovered from the rubble with serious injuries. Frankenberg dropped further bombs on Ormrod & Hardcastle's cotton mill and behind Parrott Street where extensive blast and splinter damage occurred. Next, duds aimed at the Soho Iron Works fell through the roof of Holy Trinity Church and struck business premises in Mawdsley Street and Old Hall Street South. The Zeppelin then headed away north at 12.45 am, passed close to Blackburn and dropped a last bomb near Skipton. It passed out to sea north of Whitby just after 3.00 am.

Because the town's Chief Constable had received prior warning of the raid, special constables, ambulance men and nurses were on hand to deal with its effects straightaway. The scenes of damage attracted tens of thousands of visitors in the following days, some from as far away as Liverpool. The burial of those killed next Saturday drew especially large crowds. Frankenberg and L21's own end came a couple of months later when the airship was shot down at 6.00 am on 28 November by Flight Lieutenant Cadbury and Flight Sub-Lieutenant Pulling off the Norfolk coast.

See the entry for Rawtenstall, Lancashire.

Wigan

On 12 April 1918 *Kapitänleutnant* Ehrlich, commanding L61, flew across Cheshire and turned north near Widnes. From here he discerned Wigan's smouldering blast furnaces which, not realizing just how far west he had flown, he took to be those of Sheffield. Abandoning plans to bomb Liverpool, he attacked Wigan after 11.00 pm in a raid lasting twelve minutes. Passing over the Leeds & Liverpool Canal, the Zeppelin released a stack of bombs that caused considerable damage around Darlington Street East. One which fell in Harper Street razed several terraced houses, killing two of the occupants, a Mr and Mrs Tomlinson. Further loss of life took place in Platt Lane where a mother of five, Margaret Ashbury, was in bed at the time with her four-month-old baby beside her. It appears that she raised her head to listen to the humming airship engines and was struck by a flying splinter from the explosion outside, which removed her face. At Whelley Brow bomb fragments killed an infant boy as his father carried him downstairs in search of safety, while another piece fatally wounded the father in the stomach. Nine others were injured during the attack. L61 returned home south of Bolton, leaving the Yorkshire coast near Spurn Head in the early hours of the 13th.

As so often happened, bitter recriminations followed the raid. The Town Clerk wrote in protest to the War Office about the lack of warning and unsuccessfully sued the government for compensation for those who had suffered in the town.

The first bomb released by L61 that night landed at Bold, next to a milestone on the Warrington to Prescott road, where it fractured a water main. It was the most westerly bomb dropped by the Germans in the course of the Great War. The milestone that it damaged is now displayed in Victoria Park, Widnes, accompanied by explanatory bronze plaques.

HAMPSHIRE

Portsmouth

Although Portsmouth was not actually bombed in the First World War, it was raided. This occurred on 25/26 September 1916 when *Kapitänleutnant* Mathy flew L31 over Belgium and the English Channel, intending to attack London. Under orders to exercise caution, following the loss of three German airships in the previous three weeks, Mathy declined to go against the capital because too clear visibility over the English coast would have left him vulnerable to the night fighter patrols. As an audacious alternative, however, he decided to proceed along the Channel and attempt a sortie against the naval base of Portsmouth. Flying as low as 4,000ft to drop parachute flares and pinpoint the Zeppelin's position, Mathy reached the Isle of Wight at around 11.00 pm. The raider then followed his compass north and arrived off Portsmouth within the hour, ascending to 11,000ft. Anti-aircraft fire from the docks fell short as Mathy began his attack, but the British searchlights held the

Naval Zeppelin L31, which, under **Kapitänleutnant** *Mathy, attempted to raid Portsmouth on 25/26 September 1916. Here it is seen on a naval exercise, beyond the German dreadnought SMS* **Ostfriesland.** Imperial War Museum

airship and so blinded the crew that their aim was disrupted. Although a bomb load of over 4,000kg (8,800lb) was released within two minutes and Mathy retired feeling satisfied that the city and its docks had been devastated, not a single device fell on target, or even on land. Two RNAS planes from Calshot – a Short and a White & Thompson flying boat – attempted to pursue L31 as it returned east, but they were unable to keep up with it.

British authorities charitably assumed that Mathy's bombs had spared Portsmouth because of faulty bomb releases, or that he had been on a reconnaissance mission, dumping his bombs merely to climb away. The fact that no explosions were heard from the explosives which fell in the sea would indicate that they had not been fused properly, in which case they would have been useless even if they had hit their mark.

HERTFORDSHIRE

Cheshunt

At midnight on 7/8 September 1915 Army airship LZ74, commanded by *Hauptmann* Fritz George, flew over Cheshunt bound for London. Perhaps because of ground mist, George may have mistaken the massed rows of greenhouses here for some sort of industrial installation; whatever his reason, he saw fit to unleash eighteen high explosives and twenty-seven incendiaries. The tomatoes and cucumbers below suffered terribly as a consequence, but local glaziers were guaranteed full employment. By the time LZ74 reached London only one incendiary remained in its arsenal, which George duly dropped near Fenchurch Street station in the City. This started a small fire, easily doused.

Next year, on 1/2 October, *Kapitänleutnant* Mathy dumped bombs on Cheshunt to lighten his L31 and rise beyond reach of London's AA. There was more material damage this time: as well as 6½ acres of greenhouses being demolished at the Walnut Tree nursery, nearly 350 houses sustained damage of varying degrees and the pavilion in Aubrey Ride Recreation Ground was ruined. No one was seriously hurt in the town, but for Mathy and his crew it was a different story: within the hour they were shot down and killed by Second Lieutenant Tempest in a BE2c.

The death toll for both raids on Cheshunt amounted to two chickens and a rabbit.

Cuffley

Few had heard of Cuffley before 3 September 1916, but Lieutenant William Leefe Robinson's shooting down of SL11 there put it firmly on the map. The German Army airship commanded by *Hauptmann* Schramm fell in Church Field, between St Andrew's Church at the bottom of Plough Hill and the Plough Inn at the top. (The public bar of the Plough, incidentally, was where the inquest into the deaths of the German crew was held.) As Cuffley is no longer the small village of farms and cottages that sightseers saw in 1916, but a commuter town, the sloping fields where the wreckage lay are now buried beneath an affluent housing estate. However, along the top of the steep hill runs East Ridgeway where, 200 yards from the Plough Inn, a handsome memorial to Robinson stands in a small garden behind iron railings. Unveiled on 9 June 1921, the monument is an obelisk adorned with a bronze wreath and RFC wings. Raised letters record that it was:

The Cuffley memorial to Robinson's destruction of SL11, close to where the airship plunged to earth.

Lieutenant William Leefe Robinson. He was nineteen years old when he destroyed SL11. Imperial War Museum

Erected by readers of the Daily Express *to the memory of Captain William Leefe Robinson VC, Worcs. Regt. and RFC, who on September 3 1916 above this spot brought down SL11, the first German airship destroyed on British soil.*

On the right-hand side of the monument are the words:

Captain Robinson died at Stanmore on December 31 1918, seventeen days after his return from captivity in Germany. He was taken prisoner in April 1917.

On the left-hand side is written:

The award of the Victoria Cross to Captain Robinson was thus announced in the London Gazette of September 5 1916 'For most conspicuous bravery'. He attacked an enemy airship under circumstances of great difficulty and danger, and sent it crashing to the ground as a flaming wreck. He had been in the air for more than two hours, and had previously attacked another airship during his flight.

In St Andrew's Church a brass tablet records 'the mercy of God in preserving this church & village during the fall of a burning Zeppelin within 100 yards of this spot'.

The statement is a little misleading as the present church was built in the 1960s as a replacement for the old tin church, which stood at the top of the hill close to the Robinson memorial, and where the tablet formerly hung. However, it is still easy to imagine the relief felt by the local inhabitants that night as their lives and village were spared. It is worth adding that each year on Remembrance Sunday the minister of St Andrew's graciously includes the names of the German airmen from SL11 along with the British dead.

Essendon

On the night of 2/3 September 1916 *Kapitänleutnant* Eric Sommerfeldt in L16 crossed the Norfolk coast intent on reaching London. After bombing the Great Eastern Railway's Kimberley Station, his Zeppelin arrived over Essendon shortly after 2.00 am. The presence here of two powerful searchlights made him suppose that he had reached the northern outskirts of the capital and some thirty bombs were duly released on the village. A quarter of an hour after the raid the crew of L16 witnessed the spectacular end of their compatriots in SL11, which was sent flaming to the ground at Cuffley by William Leefe Robinson. They were barely two miles away at the time and were illumined by the airship's dying glare. Not surprisingly, Sommerfeldt set off for the coast at full speed.

Of the bombs dropped on Essendon, one struck the village church, destroying the vestry and the organ and organ chamber, blowing apart the south wall of the chancel and cracking the roof over the altar, which itself was buried under rubble. Several houses were also wrecked and two sisters were felled by an explosive landing in their garden as they ran outside. Frances Mary Louis Bamford, aged twenty-six, died immediately, while her twelve-year-old sibling, Eleanor Grace, was terribly wounded along her left side. Her leg was amputated in an effort to save her but she died within the day.

The whole village was on hand to pay its respects to the sisters' funeral cortège on 6 September, their committal service being performed in the small part of the church undamaged by bombs, underlining the tragedy. The interment of the crew of SL11 at Potters Bar on the same day fuelled the anger of those who objected to the Germans being granted a military burial.

Restoration of St Mary the Virgin has since removed all traces of war damage to the church, but there is a plaque outside on the south-west corner, where the blast occurred, which records the reopening of the church on Sunday 2 September 1917. In the churchyard a single gravestone marks where the Bamford sisters are buried.

Hertford

Oberleutnant zur See Peterson, in command of L16, crossed East Anglia via Norwich and Cambridge and attacked Hertford in the evening of 13 October 1915, believing himself to be twenty miles away over East Ham and Stratford in east London. The raid began at 10.00 pm as the Zeppelin moved in a northward arc over the town. Bombs fell first on the Folly, then outside Lombard House in Bull Plain, which at the time was the Conservative Club. Four were killed at the gates, including Mr Gregory, the Borough Surveyor, as they came outside to look at the attacking Zeppelin. Explosions wrecked houses at numbers 25, 27 and 29 in Bull Plain and in Old Cross incendiaries caused fires. More houses were shattered in North Road and a soldier blown up. A high explosive falling outside the gates to Hertford County Hospital killed two workmen in Garratts Mill yard across the road and smashed the hospital's windows. With an infant killed in its cot by wall-piercing shrapnel and the death of a woman from shock elsewhere in the town, L16's thirty incendiaries and eighteen explosives were responsible for a total of nine fatalities and fifteen injured. The raid had lasted little more than two minutes.

Visitors flocked to see Hertford the next day, there being widespread rumours that it had been wiped off the map; extra police had to be summoned to maintain order in the cratered and congested streets.

Potters Bar

Kapitänleutnant Mathy in L31was shot down at Potters Bar by Second Lieutenant Tempest during the night of 1/2 October 1916. There was a narrow escape for the on-looking residents of the then village: the doomed Zeppelin fell within a short distance of their houses and would have fallen directly on top of them had a sudden gust of wind not pushed the flaming pile to safety at the last minute. Debris was scattered over a wide area. German crew members in the wreckage were burned beyond recognition, the bodies of those who leapt from the burning airship were found strewn across the meadows. The morning after, soldiers tried to guard the wreckage as the War Office wished to study its remains as intact as possible, but they were unable to prevent the villagers and hordes of visitors from taking many pieces. One of the sightseers was none other than the hero of the hour, Tempest himself, though even he had to pay the shilling charged by an enterprising farmer, Farmer Bird, to access the fields. Even more enterprising were the soldiers who passed off

The burnt remains of **Kapitänleutnant** *Mathy's L31, destroyed above Potters Bar by Second Lieutenant Tempest on 1/2 October 1916. The tree, laden with wreckage from the crash, became known as the 'Zeppelin Oak'.* Imperial War Museum

scraps of metal taken from other sources as the genuine article.

It was ironic that Mathy came down at Potters Bar, as this was where the airmen of SL11, destroyed by Robinson at Cuffley, were already buried. The vicar at Cuffley had refused to bury *Hauptmann* Schramm's crew, so they had been brought to nearby Potters Bar where the vicar of St Mary's, the Reverend E. Preston, was more charitably inclined. He volunteered to take the corpses and interred them in an unconsecrated part of the local cemetery. Father Preston received sacks of condemnatory letters, many of them obscene, for his goodwill, but he was undeterred and buried the dead of L31 next to their compatriots on 4 October. That was not the end of the controversy, however. After the war had been over for several years, the widow of Mathy, Frau Hertha, came to Potters Bar in 1926 to visit the graves. This aroused hostility from some of the locals and she was advised not to come again for her own safety. She complained to the German ambassador and he obtained an assurance from the British government that the airmen's worn wooden crosses would be replaced with proper headstones. Frau Mathy returned home pleased, unaware that the headstones did not match the graves. The graves then fell into neglect for several years, but in 1932 there began a Heroes' Day ceremony at the cemetery, attended by the German ambassador. Unfortunately, after Hitler came to power the annual service was hijacked by right-wing extremists, British as well as German, who gave offence with their Nazi salutes and swastika-decorated wreaths. Martial posturing had usurped peaceful remembrance and the local vicar refused to have anything more to do with the occasion. The advent of the Second World War ended the event altogether, of course. After that conflict a new German War Cemetery was planned for Cannock Chase in Staffordshire. The remains of the airmen of SL11 and L31 were reburied there in the 1960s. (See the entry for Cannock Chase.)

The cemetery where Mathy and his comrades first lay is on Mutton Lane. It is not advisable to visit in wet weather unless wearing appropriate footwear. The area where the Zeppelin fell has since been built over, but some of the open ground still exists in the form of Oakmere Park alongside the High Street. Bordering the opposite side of the park is Tempest Avenue, named in honour of the pilot. An oak tree that was known as the 'Zeppelin Oak', on account of the wreckage that was piled around the tree in 1916, stood for many years afterwards in what has become the private road to numbers 9 and 11. A neighbour worried about the danger posed by its dying branches later cut it down. Off The Broadway, next to the railway station, is the voluntarily run Wyllyotts Centre Local Museum. Among the displays of local history there is one relating to the Zeppelin at Potters Bar; exhibits include postcards about the event and parts of the wreckage (one especially large section of the aluminium framework), as well as a cigarette lighter made from pieces of SL11 recovered at Cuffley. Booklets about Tempest and L31 are for sale.

KENT

Ashford
During the first raid by the England Squadron, on 25 May 1917, the Gothas avoided the cloud-covered capital and attacked secondary targets in Kent. Bombs were scattered over villages and the Royal Military Canal, and when the raiders

crossed Ashford they dropped two 50kg (110lb) and four 12.5kg (27.5lb) devices. These were possibly intended for the railway works, in which case they missed. Instead, one exploded 40ft in the air above a street, killing a woman and wounding a boy and two men, while another blew up a man digging in his garden and injured three others. The *Englandgeschwader* flew on unimpeded to strike at Lympne, Hythe and Folkestone, the latter with terrible consequences for the town's inhabitants.

Earlier in the war Ashford was visited by naval Zeppelin L11, commanded by *Oberleutnant zur See* von Buttlar. Claiming to have raided Woolwich Arsenal in London on 17/18 August 1915, he had in fact crossed the coast at Herne Bay at 9.30 pm and performed a two-hour round trip over Kent. During his foray he loosed twenty-one bombs on Ashford and forty-one at Badlesmere, but not one of them proved harmful or injurious.

See the entries for Hythe, Lympne and Folkestone.

Canterbury

Westgate Museum has on display the tip of a propeller from a Gotha that crash-landed near Canterbury. The bomber was one of six that had attacked London in the early hours of 6 December 1917. It was hit by anti-aircraft fire at 5.00 am, damage to the port radiator causing the engine to overheat and finally catch fire. The Gotha came down at 5.50 am at Folly Farm, St Stephen's, where the crew, commander *Leutnant* S R Schulte, pilot *Vizefeldwebel* B Senf and gunner *Leutnant* P W Bernard, fired the aeroplane and surrendered to the local clergyman, a special constable.

Other exhibits of interest are an incendiary bomb which fell in the Canterbury area in April 1916 and a City of Canterbury 'Order as to Lights' police notice.

For the story of another Gotha that came down on 6 December 1917 see the entry for Rochford in Essex.

Chatham

Chatham, with its major naval dockyard, was a victim of the first night-time raid carried out by the England Squadron, on 3/4 September 1917. Four Gothas followed the moonlit River Medway till they reached the town, which they found fully illuminated and unguarded owing to a defensive mix up (a practice alert earlier in the evening meant that telephone warnings of a real raid, which were intended to notify the electrical department and power station to extinguish all lights at once, were not taken seriously and ignored). As well as devastating the depot – where 132 naval servicemen were killed while they slept in their hammocks in the drill hall – the Gothas also dropped bombs on Trinity School, on the cemetery, in Mallerigh Road and the High Street, flying glass causing a number of casualties.

Dover

Unsurprisingly, due to its proximity to the Continent and its role as an army and naval base, Dover was the frequent target of German raiders during the First World War. Airships and aeroplanes raided the port on over a hundred occasions, dropping 185 bombs that claimed the lives of thirteen men, seven women and three children. Dozens more were injured. Significantly, the town was where the first bomb dropped

A German postcard celebrating **Leutnant** *Karl Caspar as the first pilot to bomb Dover. In fact, although Caspar and his observer,* **Leutnant Roos,** *claimed their* **Taube** *aeroplane was the first to bomb Britain, on Christmas Day 1914, British evidence suggests they never crossed the English coast. The first bomb to have landed on these shores was actually dropped a day earlier, on 24 December, by a Friedrichshafen FF29 floatplane. The small bomb went off in a garden near Dover Castle.* Dover Museum

Dover citizens in their refuge at the Oil Mill Caves. Dover Museum

from the sky fell on British soil. This happened at 10.45 on the morning of Christmas Eve 1914 when a Friedrichshafen FF29 floatplane released its single 10kg (22lb) explosive against Dover Castle. The German missed the Castle, however, the bomb falling in a cabbage patch between the Castle and Harold Road. Windows in the neighbourhood were shattered and a man was blown out of a tree while cutting holly for Christmas decoration. He was slightly bruised, but no one else was injured in the raid. The jubilant raider returned to base, fruitlessly pursued by two British aeroplanes whose pilots were armed only with pistols.

A fragment of the bomb is displayed in Dover Museum on Market Square. The Museum also possesses numerous other items relating to the air raids, including photographs and further bomb pieces. Not all of these are on constant public display, however, some appearing only for special exhibitions.

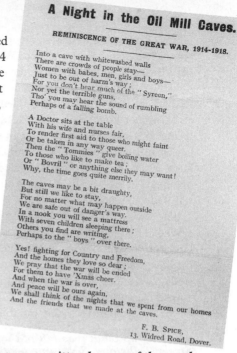

A Night in the Oil Mill Caves.

REMINISCENCE OF THE GREAT WAR, 1914-1918.

Into a cave with whitewashed walls
There are crowds of people stay—
Women with babes, men, girls and boys—
Just to be out of harm's way ;
For you don't hear much of the " Syreen,"
Nor yet the terrible guns,
Tho' you may hear the sound of rumbling
Perhaps of a falling bomb.

A Doctor sits at the table
With his wife and nurses fair,
To render first aid to those who might faint
Or be taken in any way queer.
Then the " Tommies " give boiling water
To those who like to make tea ;
Or " Bovril " or anything else they may want !
Why, the time goes quite merrily.

The caves may be a bit draughty,
But still we like to stay,
For no matter what may happen outside
We are safe out of danger's way.
In a nook you will see a mattress
With seven children sleeping there ;
Others you find are writing,
Perhaps to the " boys " over there.

Yes! fighting for Country and Freedom,
And the homes they love so dear ;
We pray that the war will be ended
For them to have 'Xmas cheer.
And when the war is over,
And peace will be ours again,
We shall think of the nights that we spent from our homes
And the friends that we made at the caves.

F. B. SPICE,
13, Widred Road, Dover.

A poem written by one of those who sheltered in the caves at Dover. It portrays people making the best of things. Dover Museum

Folkestone

The first ever Gotha raid on 25 May 1917 was intended for London, but cloud deterred Brandenburg and the England Squadron as they approached the capital and they wheeled south into Kent. Bombs fell on various towns and villages, including Ashford, Lympne and Hythe, but the German airmen reserved their deadliest attention for the resort and important base of Folkestone. As they approached it from the west the Gothas sowed six 50kg (110lb) and twenty-one 12.5kg (27.5lb) bombs on the troop camp at St Martin's Plain and Shorncliffe, killing eighteen soldiers and wounding over ninety, nearly all of them Canadian. Then they swooped in diamond formation over the town proper at 6.15 pm.

The streets were busy on this beautiful May evening: no one had taken cover. The inhabitants, who were used to army and naval exercises, had been unperturbed by the sound of explosions further away, no air raid warning had been received by the local authorities and, even if there had been, the town lacked hooters or sirens to alert the public. A more vulnerable target could not have been chosen and, although many of the bombs dropped on the town failed to detonate because their centrifugal arming devices failed, which should have been activated as they spun to earth, those that did go off were deadly.

The devices were scattered over a wide district, but most landed in the area around the Central railway station. Edward Horn, a butler, was killed in the road outside while trying to stop a runaway horse, panicked by the explosions; other bombs fell behind Kingsnorth Gardens, behind Cheriton Road and in open ground near Marten Road where two people lost their lives. A woman was killed at top of

Jointon Road and another fatality was recorded by Radnor Park. A second cluster of bombs fell around Bouverie Road West: one outside number 21 killed the occupant, Mr J Burke, hurling him across the road from his shoe repair shop and into the iron railings of the County Girls School opposite. Fifty yards away, a housemaid and two soldiers walking with her were killed by flying debris from the same blast. A bomb at 21 Manor Road caused the death of a cook in the basement, trapped beneath falling masonry. Elsewhere though, staff and guests of the Osborne Hotel, on the corner of Bouverie Road West and Christ Church Road, were fortunate enough to have evacuated the building before an explosive tore through its floors and detonated in the basement. The inside of the establishment was wrecked, but no one was badly injured.

The worst effects of the raid occurred further east in the old town centre, where a 50kg (110lb) bomb burst among a queue of shoppers outside the Stokes Brothers' Greengrocery Emporium in Tontine Street. Those on the pavement were ravaged by the blast, while the customers crowded within the shop were buried by its collapse. Bodies were torn apart, limbs and heads went missing; the later identification of corpses became a matter of surmise. Among the victims were Mr W. H. Stokes, one of the firm's partners, and his fourteen-year-old son. Townspeople outside the

Clearing up what was left of the Stokes Brothers' greengrocery in Tontine Street, Folkstone. Sixty-one people died when a bomb fell outside the shop during the first air raid on England by Gothas, 25 May 1917. Kent Arts & Libraries (Folkstone Library)

drapers on the other side of the road were also killed. Blast damage extended up and down the street and a ruptured gas main threatened further devastation before the fire was extinguished. Councillor John Jones who had been sitting in front of the *Brewery Tap* pub, next door to the greengrocers, when the bomb went off wrote afterwards:

> *The sight was appalling, and beggars description. The busy crowded street, all life, was, in ten seconds, transformed into a shambles. No scene at the battlefield could have been more frightful.*

The single bomb in Tontine Street was responsible for the deaths of sixty-one, of whom twenty-seven were children. In all, seventy-one persons died and ninety-six were injured. The attack lasted barely ten minutes, yet it was the worst to befall Kent in the war.

Folkestone had been unscathed for the first three years of conflict and, prior to this raid, the community wrongly thought that it might remain immune to 'frightfulness' because of pre-war links with Germany over a ship, the *Grosser Kurfürst*, which sank off Folkestone in 1878, many of its seamen being buried locally. The sense of betrayal added to locals' bitterness at the Hun, but some anger was reserved for their own government and its failure to defend them. A deputation from the Town Council duly went to London the following week to demand better protection from Lord French, Commander-in-Chief of Home Forces. Unwilling to rely on the government, however, Folkestone quickly purchased a siren on its own behalf. Town committees argued back and forth about the future advisability of public shelters, so-called 'shelterists' being opposed by those who pointed out that the supposed places of refuge simply were not bombproof. Despite these reservations, in the following months numbers of jumpy townsfolk hung around the designated places waiting for the first hint of a siren. Happily, the shelters were never tested, for, although Folkestone experienced alarms in the last year of the war, it was not raided again.

Today, remembering the tragic events of May 1917, there is a small plaque on a metal post, located halfway along Tontine Street next to the Brewery Tap. It marks the site of Messrs Stokes' greengrocers where so many lives were lost – a site that has not been built on since the shop's destruction. Folkestone Museum, nearby on Grace Hill, has a small display about the First World War air raids and contains a piece of 'Zeppelin Wire' – taken from the Schütte-Lanz, SL11, brought down by Robinson at Cuffley – sold in aid of the Red Cross.

See the entries for Ashford, Hythe and Lympne.

Gravesend

Naval Zeppelin L10 meandered down the Thames estuary on 4 June 1915, circling the Isle of Sheppey and scattering a few bombs on Sittingbourne before continuing west to Gravesend. The confused airship commander, *Kapitänleutnant* Hirsch, carried out the raid wrongly supposing his victim to be Harwich naval base, and the lights of London visible to the west to be those of Ipswich. As the Zeppelin performed a figure of eight above the town, bombs wrecked several houses along Windmill Street, shattered windows in Wingfield Road and set fire to a property in Peppercroft Street. An explosive demolished two residences in Wrotham Road and buried the five occupants beneath rubble, but they were dug out without serious injury. Bombs next fell behind Woodville Terrace, and then Brandon Street was targeted, where lamps around a hole in the street and a watchman's coke brazier may have been taken for a railway station. An incendiary burned down a stable, killing a pair of horses, while further along the road a bomb damaged houses and a woman was struck in the face by flying metal. In Cobham Street a dud penetrated one property all the way through to its basement, and behind Bath Street an incendiary set fire to garden fencing. A firebomb on the nightnurses' quarters at the General Hospital in Bath Street caused a more serious blaze, but luckily for the women they were all on duty at the time and so no one was there. A final explosive fell in front of the Yacht Club, which was being used as a VAD military hospital. The blast collapsed its ceilings and rendered the entire place uninhabitable, but the only personal injury was a nurse's dislocated shoulder.

Despite the fact that no one was killed in the raid, those who could stayed away from Gravesend for several months afterwards. Fearing a repeat assault, they only moved back as they realized that places such as Meopham and Southfleet were just as vulnerable. The Zeppelins never did return to Gravesend, but in the summer of 1917 the England Squadron dropped bombs on the golf links and on 31 October/1 November that year Gothas damaged houses in Prospect Place. At number 20 a Mrs Porter and her two daughters had a narrow escape when they abandoned their kitchen to huddle under the stairs, barely moments before an incendiary gutted the room.

Hawkinge
The voluntarily run Kent Battle of Britain Museum may be found at the former Second World War airbase on the A260 between Folkestone and Canterbury. Although dedicated to the struggle of 1940, exhibits do include a few Gotha and Zeppelin fragments, along with other Great War material. These are displayed in the Armoury building.

Hythe
Hythe was one of the Kentish towns bombed by Brandenburg's *Englandgeschwader* when they made their first strike on 25 May 1917. More than a dozen of their 'eggs' fell on the town, causing minor structural damage, but killing two inhabitants. Mrs Amy Parker was killed in Ormonde Road by a bomb splinter through her heart; Daniel Lyth, the verger of the parish church, received fatal shrapnel wounds to his leg as he, the vicar and his wife stood on St Leonard's church steps.

See the entries for Ashford, Folkestone and Lympne.

Lympne
On 13 October 1915 L14 (*Kapitänleutnant der Reserve* Böcker) flew over Kent and reached the English Channel. The commander took this to be the Thames and, finding Hythe, judged that to be Woolwich. At least four bombs were released near Lympne, which fell on the Canadian Army camp at Otterpool at 10.15 pm. Fifteen of the soldiers quartered there were killed and another eleven were injured. Böcker's Zeppelin departed north via Tunbridge Wells, Croydon and south-east London.

Gothas making their first sortie on England hit the RFC airfield at Lympne on 25 May 1917. Three 50kg (110lb) and nineteen 12.5kg (27.5lb) explosives caused craters at the base, but no men were hurt or aeroplanes damaged before the raiders passed on to Hythe and Folkestone.

See the entries for Ashford, Folkestone and Hythe.

Margate

Margate was bedevilled by air raids and alarms, especially from 1917 when the Gothas entered the German service. The inhabitants of this Thanet town, however, had the satisfaction of seeing several raiders brought down in the war. One of these was L15 as it returned from a raid on London. The German naval Zeppelin, commanded by *Kapitänleutnant* Breithaupt, had experienced difficulty maintaining height and fell prey to anti-aircraft batteries along the Thames Estuary. They punctured its gas cells and it came down with a broken back in the sea off Margate, near the Kentish Knock Light Vessel, at 12.15 am on 1 April 1916. One crew member drowned, but HMS *Vulture* rescued the other sixteen. An attempt was made to tow the airship into harbour but it sank off Westgate. As the first airship to have been downed by Home Defence, different batteries, as well as RFC pilot Second Lieutenant Brandon, who attacked the airship as it dropped into the sea, were keen to claim the kill; the credit was divided.

During a raid on 22 August 1917 one Gotha nose-dived into the sea a mile offshore of the resort as a result of combined AA and fire from British aeroplanes; the only survivor was *Unteroffizier* Bruno Schneider, the gunner. Another Gotha was sent out of control by the explosion of AA beneath it. As it fell it burst into flames and broke up into three pieces, the main part coming down at Vincent Farm, near

A mobile searchlight of the RNAAS on service at Margate in the summer of 1915. Imperial War Museum

Manston. This time there were no survivors. Onlookers heartily cheered both kills, but the remaining Gothas claimed the lives of eight and injured a further twenty-two in the town.

Margate Local History Museum in the Old Town Hall on Market Street has a display about Margate in the First World War and exhibits include aluminium struts and gasbag fragments taken from L15. Alongside are photographs of air raid damage and a 'War Souvenir' listing all the raids in the Thanet area. The Museum also possesses fragments of the Vincent Farm Gotha. Not far from the Museum, in Trinity Square, is Margate's War Memorial. The town's eighteen-raid casualties, including five soldiers, are recorded separately on the rear side.

For more details of the Vincent Farm Gotha see the following entry for RAF Manston History Museum.

RAF Manston History Museum

Manston was established as a RNAS base in late May 1916, initially provided with Sopwith 1½ Strutters. A Handley Page Training School was also stationed there from December, and in April 1917 the flight was increased from six to nine aircraft and anti-aircraft guns established in defence of the base. A number of Manston pilots distinguished themselves during the Gotha daylight offensive. On the morning of 7 July 1917 the Squadron Commander, C. H. Butler, and others from the base intercepted Gothas returning from a raid on London. Butler in a Sopwith Triplane pursued two enemy aeroplanes for half an hour and engaged them at close quarters off the Belgian coast, bringing down the first in the sea. Flight Sub-Lieutenant Rowan H. Daly in another Triplane shot down an unspecified German aeroplane in flames in the same area (probably a fighter escort for the returning bombers), while Flight Lieutenant J. E. Scott in a Camel attacked a Gotha thirty-five miles north-east of North Foreland and sent it spinning into the sea. All three Manston men were credited with kills the following day; Butler was awarded a bar to his DSO and Daly and Scott received DSCs.

The following month, on Wednesday, 22 August 1917, Flight Lieutenant Arthur Frank Brandon (not to be confused with RFC pilot Alfred de Bathe Brandon), flying a Camel, engaged several Gothas and may have been responsible for the one which

Sopwith Camels at RAF Manston during the Gotha offensive. Imperial War Museum

came down close to the base at Vincent Farm, Vincent Lane. The bomber spiralled to earth in flames, one side's wings falling at Garlinge and an engine on Hengrove golf links. All three crewmen were killed, the observer *Oberleutnant* Echart Fulda, pilot *Unteroffizier* Heinrich Schildt and gunner *Vizefeldwebel* Ernst Eickelkamp. They were buried with full military honours at dawn in Margate Cemetery by a RNAS detail and later removed to Cannock Chase German War Cemetery. Brandon made no positive claim for the destruction of their Gotha, the first to be shot down on British soil, and it was adjudged that AA probably was responsible after his attack. However, Brandon contributed to the destruction of another Gotha in the sea off Margate that morning and was awarded the DSC for his efforts, though he died before he received the medal when another pilot descended on to his plane in midair on 26 October 1917. He was buried at Minster.

RAF Manston History Museum has an extensive display about Manston and the First World War air raids, some of it on loan from the nearby Powell Cotton Museum at Quex Park, Birchington-on-Sea. Among the exhibits are pieces of the Vincent Farm Gotha, including a propeller tip, a square of camouflage fabric, souvenir matchboxes made from recovered metal, a main spar and other sections. Other items are RFC and RNAS cap and shoulder badges, a mounted propeller section of Zeppelin L15, a silver pocket watch that belonged to Major Edward Mannock (the RAF's greatest ace with seventy-three kills, killed in action on 26 July 1918) and replicas of Brandon's medals. There are also photographs documenting Manston in the Great War. One hangar survives in good order from the time, but this is not open to the public.

Manston continued in military service to the Second World War and after, and today is a commercial airport. The RAF Manston History Museum is on Manston Road, opposite the Spitfire and Hurricane Memorial Museum.

Ramsgate

Ramsgate's vulnerable position on the south-east coast made it one of the most frequently attacked towns in the country, the combined tally of air raids and naval bombardments amounting to 119. Its population halved during the war as a result.

Its first aerial assault took place in the early hours of 17 May 1915 when *Hauptmann* Linnarz's LZ38 dropped around twenty bombs. One struck the Bull & George Hotel in the High Street, where it penetrated several storeys and exploded on the first floor. The building was gutted and two of those injured inside later died of their wounds. Further damage occurred in Albion Place and East Cliff, but there were no more casualties. On its way out to sea the Army Zeppelin was caught by Dover searchlights – the first time that an enemy airship was so illuminated – and chased by RNAS Flight Sub-Lieutenant Redford H Mulock in an Avro 504c. LZ38 soon rose out of range, however.

The next serious raid happened on Sunday, 19 March 1916. Four aeroplanes of *See Flieger Abteilung* 1, based at Zeebrugge, made a series of attacks on the Kent coastal towns, a pair of the German seaplanes depositing ten bombs on Ramsgate at 2.00 pm. One of the devices obliterated a car and its driver close to St Luke's Church; another exploded in the midst of a party of children walking to Sunday School. Five of the youngsters, aged between four and twelve, were killed and nine injured.

The worst raid in terms of material destruction occurred the following year, on 17 June, when naval Zeppelin L42 dropped two or three bombs at two o'clock in the

*The Bull & George Hotel in Ramsgate, after a Zeppelin raid on 17 May 1915.
A bomb dropped by* **Hauptmann** *Erich* **Linnarz,** *in LZ38, gutted the interior
and fatally injured two people.* Imperial War Museum

morning. Although the commander of the airship, *Kapitänleutnant* Martin Dietrich, might have been disappointed to discover that he had hit Ramsgate instead of Dover, he would have been gratified that one of his 300kg (660lb) devices landed on the Royal Navy ammunition dump in the harbour. This resulted in a series of explosions that utterly wrecked the naval base, damaged hundreds of houses and broke thousands of windows. However, only three persons lost their lives, all of them in Albert Street. Two of them were a husband and wife, buried beneath the ruins of their house; although the woman was extricated alive, she died the following afternoon from her injuries. Fourteen other civilians and two servicemen were also hurt by the incident. Ramsgate's AA batteries and fourteen searchlights opened up in immediate response, but the black-bellied Zeppelin eluded them. L42's other bomb (or bombs) fell in the sea.

Another notable raid was that of 22 August 1917. The assailants this time were Gothas, who dropped twenty-eight bombs within a square mile of the High Street. One 50kg (110lb) bomb fell in Military Road, next to the harbour, and struck a store where people were sheltering from the attack, killing six men and a child. The deaths of two Canadian soldiers elsewhere in the town brought the total of dead to nine; twenty-one were injured.

Unfortunately, if not unsurprisingly, anti-German resentment endured the Armistice in Ramsgate. In 1920, when a German ship unloaded coal at the port, locals rioted and had to be forcibly restrained from plundering the vessel.

Sheerness

As a garrison town and naval port Sheerness suffered several raids in the First World War. The worst of these occurred on the early evening of 5 June 1917 when Gothas targeted the army camps and dockyard. Bombing began at 6.30 pm and lasted less than five minutes. Rifleman Maurice Gower afterwards wrote to his sister Flo about this 'bit of excitement':

> *I was seated in a picture palace when they were over Sheerness dropping their bombs, the house was not very full and the first instance we had of a raid, was the shutting down of the lights; they opened all the doors, then we could hear the bombs dropping all around the place – they seemed to be coming nearer and were coming down pretty thick.*

Interestingly enough, the cinemagoers were a sanguine lot: 'nobody got very excited, the audience being mostly sailors'. But outside in the busy streets there was mayhem.

Ten servicemen were killed and twenty-five injured in the raid; civilian casualties were three dead and nine injured. Anti-aircraft fire was probably accountable for the Gotha which fell in a spin in the sea off Barton's Point; the pilot *Vizefeldwebel* Erich Kluck was drowned, his observer *Leutnant* Hans Francke died the day after being picked up, but the gunner *Unteroffizier* Georg Schumacher survived with a broken leg. The British press trumpeted erroneous claims that other enemy aeroplanes had also been shot down – the *Daily Express* declared half the German raiders that day were destroyed and looked forward to them returning for some more.

The War Memorial in Sheerness is inscribed with the names of the citizens and Army and Navy servicemen who lost their lives in air raids at Sheerness. The memorial is of Portland stone, the base surmounted by a figure of Liberty bearing a flaming torch. It is situated opposite the train station, at the junction of the High Street, Bridge Street and the new Millennium Way.

LANCASHIRE

Rawtenstall

Around midnight on 25/26 September 1916 naval Zeppelin L21 (*Oberleutnant zur See* Frankenberg) dropped an incendiary bomb near Height Side House. It failed to go off, as did a high explosive that fell behind Lea Bank House. Subsequent bombs did explode, but these produced only craters until, having crossed the town from east to west, the Zeppelin entered Rossendale valley and damaged a sewage works, train track and houses near the level crossing with a series of explosives and incendiaries. Frankenberg continued to the village of Holcombe where structural damage was caused in Helmshore Road to the village school, the Lower House inn (now the Shoulder of Mutton) and the post office across the road (now a private house). Bombs in nearby Ramsbottom partially demolished a mineral works there and an incendiary on Greenmount set alight a cottage. L21 then proceeded to Bolton where it did most damage that night.

The incendiary which fell harmlessly and intact near Height Side House is now on display at Whitaker Park Museum in Rawtenstall, while the three buildings that were hit in Holcombe still bear the scars of the explosions.

See the entry for Bolton, Greater Manchester.

LEICESTERSHIRE

Loughborough

Ten people were killed and eight injured in Loughborough during an air raid in the early evening of 31 January 1916. Twenty-seven 50kg (110lb) bombs fell on the town, dropped by *Kapitänleutnant* Stabbert, in command of Zeppelin L20. Most damage befell The Rushes, Ashby Square and Empress Road, where houses were demolished. It seems that the town's streetlamps were alight prior to the raid, which would explain how Stabbert targeted Loughborough, but many locals were not satisfied by such a simple solution – they preferred something more sinister. Some asserted that a luminous arrow pointing to the town had been painted on top of the Beeches Road bridge by a mysterious figure; others claimed that the Zeppelin was guided towards Loughborough, and specifically to the Herbert Morris firm of crane makers, by the car headlights of one Frank Bastert, a German who was former partner in the business (notwithstanding the fact that Herr Bastert had returned to Germany before the war).

In Loughborough today there are several reminders of this First World War air raid. In The Rushes a dull metal plaque in a wooden frame hangs on the wall between two small shops on the western side of the street, opposite the bus stop. A replacement for the original, unveiled in 1918, it informs passers-by:

Opposite this tablet at a spot indicated by a granite square there fell on the 31st January 1918 a bomb discharged from a German airship which exploded, causing the death of several persons, injuring many others and doing great damage to the surrounding property.

144

Naval Zeppelin L20, which raided Loughborough on 31 January 1916, killing ten and injuring eight. Its commander was Kapitänleutnant *Franz Stabbert.* Royal Air Force Museum

The square stone referred to is set in the road on the other side and is incised with a German cross. A modern plaque, similar to the one in The Rushes, may be found in Empress Road. It is fixed to the side wall of a house, in between where Judges Street and Thomas Street join Empress Road. Once again, a stone cut with a German cross marks the spot in the street where a bomb landed. There is no memorial in Ashby Square, but the Crown and Cushion pub that was slightly damaged in the raid is still a going concern.

In Queen's Park there is the War Memorial Tower and Loughborough Carillon. This was built in 1923 by public subscription and the bells cast in the town at Taylor's Bell Foundry. As well as offering visitors a fine view of Loughborough, the tower also displays items relevant to the 1916 air raid. On the ground floor there is a small display about the event and just inside the entrance hangs an original air raid commemorative plaque. Upstairs in the War Memorial Museum, on the second floor, pieces of bomb casing from the raid are exhibited in a glass case. Of further interest, on the first floor there is a piece of bomb dropped in 1917 on members of the Leicestershire Yeomanry while they were encamped at Shorncliffe, near Folkestone, during the first Gotha raid on the country.

See the entries for Ilkeston in Derbyshire and Burton upon Trent in Staffordshire, which Stabbert's L20 bombed after Loughborough. For other Midlands towns and cites that were raided by Zeppelins of the Naval Airship Division on the same night see Derby, and Birmingham and Walsall in the West Midlands.

LINCOLNSHIRE

Boston

Despite its position on the east coast and the fact that a Zeppelin had flown over the town earlier in the war, a blackout was only half-heartedly maintained in Boston. This proved fatal for one young man. On 2/3 September 1916 Tom Oughton, a special constable and lock keeper of the Grand Sluice Bridge, was keeping watch outside his house on Haven Bank. Having been warned of an imminent raid, he ordered a passing fish merchant called 'Dinghy' Clark to put out his flashlight, but Clark ignored the order and an argument broke out. The sound of raised voices brought Oughton's sons and pregnant wife outside just as there was the whistle of a falling bomb, which struck a stone pier of the Grand Sluice. Splinters from the blast injured Tom Oughton and his wife, but killed one son, also named Tom, who died within minutes of chest wounds; close by, a railway gatekeeper at the Grand Sluice signal box was also hurt, as well as another railway man. Whether or not the light of the flashlight was to blame for drawing the Zeppelin's fire, the uncooperative Clark was unharmed.

Other bombs dropped on the town landed in Witham Bank West, at the entrance to the gas works, and at the back of houses in Fydell Street. The Zeppelin responsible was L23, under the command of *Kapitänleutnant* Wilhelm Ganzel; it was not SL11, which William Leefe Robinson famously destroyed above Cuffley later that night, as many aggrieved Bostonians had hoped. Ganzel returned without incident to Nordholz, thinking he had assaulted Norwich. In Boston the authorities henceforward enforced a more rigid blackout.

Cleethorpes

On the night of 31 March/1 April 1916, when several naval Zeppelins set out for a raid on London (and L15 was brought down in the sea), *Kapitänleutnant* Martin Dietrich, commanding L22, decided to cut short his journey due to engine trouble and attack the Humber estuary as an alternative. He hoped, and thought, he had hit the port of Grimsby, but struck neighbouring Cleethorpes instead. One of L22's bombs landed on the town's Baptist Church Hall, Alexandra Road, with devastating effect. Eighty-four soldiers of the 3rd Battalion (Special Reserve), Manchester Regiment, had been billeted there just hours after arriving in the area to bolster the Humber's defences against invasion. The explosion demolished the walls and ceiling of the hall and killed twenty-seven of the men instantaneously; of the fifty-three wounded, five died later. Only four soldiers were unharmed: these were rescued from a cellar they had stolen into to play cards.

Further bombs fell in Sea View Street and Cambridge Street. The raid prompted some of the town's inhabitants to leave for the countryside for the duration of the war, but two locals who fled Cleethorpes did so against their will. These were the local postmaster and a café owner who were wrongly suspected of being of German origin, and became the focus of rumours about spies having signalled to the raider. Twenty-four of those who were killed at the Baptist Church are buried together in Cleethorpes Cemetery, Bentley Street; those victims not buried here were taken back to their own parishes. A stone memorial surmounted by a cross was raised by

Cleethorpes Baptist Church Hall, demolished on 1 April 1916 by **Kapitanleutnant** *Martin Dietrich, commanding L22. Of eighty-four men of the Manchester Regiment billeted there when the bomb went off, thirty-two died immediately or soon after.* Lincoln Central Library, Leonard W. Pye Collection

public subscription close to the western edge of the burial ground, bearing the names of thirty-one of the dead. It stands on a low mound, on the front of which is a shield-shaped stone dedicated by Cleethorpes Baptist Church, quoting 1 Corinthians 15:54: 'Death is swallowed up in victory'. At a service of remembrance to mark the 85th anniversary of the raid, on 1 April 2001, 'The Manchester Chapel' was dedicated at the Baptist Church as a further commemoration of the fallen.

See the following entry for *Kapitänleutnant* Martin Dietrich's second attempt against Grimsby.

Grimsby

It was a Grimsby fishing trawler, the *King Stephen*, which was involved in the controversial decision to abandon the crew of L19 in the North Sea in early 1916. *Kapitänleutnant* Loewe's Zeppelin was returning from a raid on Burton upon Trent and the Midlands on 31 January when it experienced engine and wireless failure and drifted low close to Holland. Dutch soldiers opened fire with rifles at the airship on the late afternoon of 1 February, possibly crippling it altogether, and a south wind sprung up to push the Zeppelin back out to sea and towards Britain. When it eventually came down, Loewe's crew discarded the gondolas to try to keep it afloat and made some sort of basic shelter for themselves on the slowly sinking envelope. German destroyers were sent to search for L19 but found only an abandoned fuel tank, and the Zeppelin was not seen again until it was sighted 110 miles off

Britain was vilified in the German press when the captain of a Grimsby trawler refused to rescue the crew of crippled Zeppelin L19, which had come down in the North Sea. The airship, commanded by Kapitänleutnant Odo Loewe, had been returning from a raid on 31 January/1 February 1916; all on board eventually drowned. This cartoon, depicting the Bishop of London who had defended the decision to abandon the shipwrecked Germans, appeared in Lustige Blätter. It was entitled 'And the Levite passed by...', a reference to Luke 10:32 and the tale of the Good Samaritan.

Flamborough Head by the *King Stephen* at 6.00 am on 2 February. Captain Martin refused to rescue the sixteen stricken Germans despite their pleas and offers of money, for the apparent reason that they might overpower his crew of eight, even though they were surely too cold and exhausted. The English skipper reported the wreck next day when his vessel returned to port, but by then assistance was too late. Loewe's last report was washed up in a bottle in Sweden and indicates that his craft sank soon after the *King Stephen* had left. Understandably, the episode occasioned much bitterness in Germany; remarks made by the Bishop of London caused particular offence when he publicly defended the actions of the skipper in letting the men drown. Some satisfaction was later gleaned, however, when a German torpedo boat sunk the *King Stephen* on 23 April and its fishermen were imprisoned in Germany.

During the Great War Grimsby received the attention of various naval airship commanders, but all missed the town proper. The closest any of them came was when *Kapitänleutnant* Martin Dietrich, in command of Zeppelin L22, attacked on the night of 23/24 September 1916. He was unsure of his bearings and his fourteen bombs fell without harm on the village of Scartho, today a suburb of Grimsby. On the side wall of business premises at 46 Louth Road there is still a plaque that celebrates the preservation of 'the inhabitants of this village from death and injury', and commends the reader to observe Psalm 91. Appropriately, verses 5-6 of this Psalm state:

> *Thou shalt not be afraid of the terror by night, nor for the arrow that flieth by day; for the pestilence that walketh in darkness, nor for the destruction that wasteth at noonday.*

In the parish churchyard there is another memorial raised in thanksgiving, a marble column topped by an urn, bestowed by a Mr J Grantham.

Although Dietrich hurt no one on this occasion, an earlier attempt to raid Grimsby on 31 March/1 April 1916 claimed the lives of over thirty men of the Manchester Regiment, billeted a couple of miles away at Cleethorpes. (See the preceding entry for Cleethorpes.)

Lincoln

L14, commanded by *Hauptmann* Manger, approached Lincoln on the night of 23/24 September 1916. It was repelled from an attack on the city by anti-aircraft fire from Canwick Hill and bombed Washingborough to the east instead. Four bombs damaged windows and a pear tree, other devices fell close to the River Witham which runs alongside the village. It was conjectured afterwards that the German airship had targeted the Grimsby to Lincoln train, which it presumed had arrived at a station when the driver, who in turn had spotted the Zeppelin, brought it to a halt in a nearby cutting.

Although none of L14's bombs claimed any lives, tragedy occurred next day when Lincolners flocked to Washingborough to visit the scene of the raid. The ferry across the Witham was being pulled that Sunday by sixty-nine-year-old George Moore, who struggled to cope with its weight. On one occasion, as sightseers made the return journey, the overcrowded ferry grounded in shallows. When it listed to one side the occupants surged to the other, causing it to capsize. Of the twenty-five on board, two boys of seven and seventeen became trapped beneath the vessel and drowned: George Nelson and Ernest Robinson. Another person, Fred Cooke, was dragged underwater by the weight of his bomb-fragment-filled pockets and passed out, and there he would have died undiscovered, but that someone noticed him when they stood on his face and pulled him out in the nick of time.

In St John's Church in Washingborough there are eight stained glass Zeppelin Memorial windows in commemoration of the air raid, four along each side of the clerestory, above the nave. Put in by Rector William Burland during restorations later on in the First World War, each refers to Zeppelins L30 and L32. Although neither of these airships ever bombed Washingborough or Lincoln, L32, commanded by *Oberleutnant zur See* Peterson, is relevant because it was shot down by Second Lieutenant Frederick Sowrey on the same night that Washingborough was raided. L30, under the now *Kapitänleutnant* von Buttlar, was involved in the attack on Britain that night, but did nothing memorable; the airship was never destroyed by enemy action and was withdrawn from service in November 1917. It is probable, then, that L30 was a mistake for L33, the Zeppelin commanded by *Kapitänleutnant der Reserve* Böcker which came down at Little Wigborough on the morning of 24 September 1916. Confusion about which airship was which was common during and after the war when details were either unknown or classified.

See the entries for Great Burstead and Little Wigborough, in Essex, for the respective accounts of L32 and L33's demise.

Scunthorpe

Scunthorpe was raided on 31 January 1916 by *Kapitänleutnant* Mathy in L13. His Zeppelin was undetected until its engines were heard directly overhead at 10.45 pm. When residents realized what was going on many of them fled the town for the countryside in their nightclothes, which action led to cases of pneumonia, some reportedly fatal. The raid itself lasted eight and a half minutes, during which time twenty high explosives and over fifty incendiaries fell on the town.

An explosive falling in Ravendale Street blew in the backs of four houses and slightly damaged nearby properties. Numerous incendiaries landed around the Glebe pit and a bomb detonated in a paddock on Trafford Street. Another explosive struck Wheatlands, then an incendiary fell through a roof in Trent Cottages, where eighty-six-year-old Mrs Markham was about to retire for the night. The widow doused it with remarkable aplomb before a neighbour arrived and threw it out of the window. Subsequent bombs fell on the foundry at Trent Iron Company works and the North Lincoln works yard. Devices on Redbourn Hill Iron Works caused the death of two employees, Thomas Danson and Jack Cyril Wright, and damaged the engine and boiler house. Frodingham Iron and Steel works and a chemical plant were spared as L13 flew over them, but the following bomb exploded in a siding where it injured four railway workers. More weapons landed in Lindsey yard and a device near Dawes Lane claimed the night's third victim, Wilkinson Benson. After this, the Zeppelin departed in the direction of Ashby whence it had come.

At the time of the raid the lights in Scunthorpe's houses were low and the street lamps were not lit. What had caught Mathy's eye was a fire at a slagheap near the iron works, burning as a warning to railway engines tipping slag not to go over the end of a bank.

See the entry for Stoke-on-Trent in Staffordshire, which Mathy raided earlier that evening.

NORFOLK

Caister-on-Sea

In Holy Trinity Cemetery lies Miss Martha Taylor, one of the two first victims of an air raid on Britain. She was killed in Great Yarmouth by a bomb from L3 and is buried in the Southern Section of the main cemetery, on the western side of the High Street. Her grave is located behind the brick Chapel. Instead of a headstone a low kerb marks her resting place: this is barely visible today beneath overgrowing grass. Along the outside of the right-hand kerbstone one may still read the faint inscription, which includes a quote from *The Book of Common Prayer's* Burial of the Dead:

> Mary Martha Taylor fell a victim to an air raid on Great Yarmouth January 19th 1915 in her 73rd year. 'In the midst of life we are in death'.

The left-hand kerb remembers her twin sister, Jane Eliza, who died several years later, on 15 January 1918. The front and back kerbstones read 'In loving memory of'.

See the entry for Great Yarmouth.

Dereham

Kapitänleutnant der Reserve Böcker, in L14, intended to attack London on 8 September 1915, but engine trouble restricted his operations to East Anglia. He attacked Dereham, which he and his crew took for Norwich, shortly before 9.00 pm. Approaching from the west, the Zeppelin may have been drawn to the town by soldiers atop Bylaugh Church tower who were said to have been signalling to servicemen on other church towers in the district. Whatever the cause, Church Farm was bombed on the outskirts, and within the town a conflagration erupted in Market Place, caused by an incendiary falling on an oil store at the back of the ironmonger's. Maroons to summon the fire brigade were kept at the King's Arms Hotel, but everyone there was too busy cowering in the cellar to fire one. In the end, a shopkeeper from nearby arrived and took charge of the situation.

In Church Street bombs damaged numerous shops and banks, and the White Lion pub was completely destroyed; a couple having a quiet drink there at the time, Harry and Sylvia Johnson, were gravely injured. Further along, a house in front of the Corn Hall was levelled by a high explosive. Its collapse claimed the life of an unfortunate soldier just as he dashed inside in search of shelter, while the occupier, Mr Catton, who had left the house seconds before to see what was going on, survived. The blast and shrapnel killed James Taylor, Harry Patterson and Lance Corporal Alfred Pomeroy in the street.

The Zeppelin continued on to Bylaugh releasing several more bombs in its wake. Then it doubled back over Dereham and away home. The town had been defenceless against the raider. The next day a bundle of German newspapers that had been parachuted down were discovered in a field near Scarning, along with an officer's cap, evidently dropped by mistake. In town, sightseers thronged the damaged streets hampering repair work.

Dilham

Nineteen explosives and twenty-six incendiaries fell on this village on the night of 24/25 April 1916. They were dropped by L11 (*Korvettenkapitän* Schütze). Although there was little physical damage to the houses, an elderly woman died of shock.

Great Yarmouth

Great Yarmouth has the distinction of being the first victim of the German Zeppelins. For that it is indebted to *Kapitänleutnant* Hans Fritz, the commander of L3, when he arrived over Norfolk far short of his intended target in the Humber area, on the evening of Tuesday, 19 January 1915. After dropping one bomb in a meadow at Ormesby, Fritz began his bomb run on the port at 8.25 pm. The Zeppelin flew in a north-south direction 5,000ft above the town, using parachute flares to illuminate the ground. The raid lasted ten long minutes, during which a number of high explosives and incendiary bombs were released.

Soldiers show off part of a bomb that fell in Crown Road, Great Yarmouth. It was dropped by **Kapitänleutnant** *Fritz, in L3, during the first airship raid on Britain, 19 January 1915.* **Imperial War Museum**

The first bomb dropped on Great Yarmouth fell in Norfolk Square, a garden behind Albemarle Road; the second landed on a stable at the rear of 78 Crown Road; the third landed in St Peter's Plain where the first ever casualties of an air raid on Britain occurred. The two killed were Samuel Smith and Martha Taylor. Mr Smith was caught in a hail of bomb fragments that tore away part of his head; Miss Taylor was mutilated by the blast and her clothes ripped off. Craters were opened in the road, houses were wrecked and the windows of St Peter's Church were blown in. Other bombs fell at the corner of South Quay and Friars Lane, Southgate Road, in the river, damaging a steamer, and near the grandstand of the old racecourse on South Denes. Despite the dead and injured, there were many lucky escapes that night as the town's citizens stood in the streets listening to the Zeppelin's progress and trying to make it out against the night sky.

The next day the government and press downplayed the raid, at the same time as denouncing it. In Germany, on the other hand, where L3 arrived back at Fuhlsbüttel after almost twenty-three hours in the air, the raid's significance was inflated, with postcards concocted from fabricated photographs published depicting the Zeppelin bombing Great Yarmouth's Town Hall. Meanwhile Mr Smith and Miss Taylor were quietly laid to rest, in private ceremonies, away from public attention. Mr Smith was buried in an unmarked grave in the Old Cemetery; Miss Taylor was buried at Caister. The Coroner investigating their deaths told the inquest:

> The unfortunate man and woman were victims of so-called warfare – but I do not call it so. It is the offspring of German culture.

Later in the war Great Yarmouth had the satisfaction of having some revenge on the Zeppelins of the German Navy. It was from the RNAS base just south of the town, in open ground next to the foreshore at South Denes, that Flight Lieutenant Cadbury helped bring down L21 on 28 November 1916; it was also from here that Flight Lieutenant Christopher J. Galpin and Captain Robert Leckie took off in a

The RNAS base at South Denes, south of Great Yarmouth. Imperial War Museum

The Curtiss H12 Flying Boat that destroyed Zeppelin L22, 14 May 1917. Flying from RNAS South Denes, it was piloted by Captain Robert Leckie, with Flight Lieutenant Christopher Galpin as the bow-gunner. Radio signals from the Zeppelin had given away its location on patrol in the German Bight, and not expecting any British aeroplane to know where it was or to come so far out to sea, its crew were unprepared when the H12 attacked. Imperial War Museum

Curtiss H12 Flying Boat and destroyed L22 over the North Sea on 14 May 1917. Finally, it was from the South Denes base that Leckie and Cadbury were to take off together in a DH4 on 5 August 1918 to snag the greatest prize of the war, Strasser in L70, having a go at L65 immediately afterwards. This was the last air raid on the country, Zeppelin or otherwise. It may be said, then, that air raids in the First World War began and ended with Great Yarmouth.

Today, recalling the first Zeppelin raid, a plaque above the front door of 25 St Peter's Plain, since restored, declares it 'The First House in Great Britain to be damaged by a Zeppelin Air Raid 19th January 1915'. Nearby is St Peter's Church (now Greek Orthodox) which was also damaged in the raid. Norfolk Square is a private garden but can be seen from the roadside; the bomb fell behind 6 Albemarle Road, now a hotel.

The Great Yarmouth Maritime Museum on Marine Parade has various exhibits relating to the First World War air raids, including a souvenir fragment of the bomb that landed in St Peter's Plain, high explosive and incendiary bombs, scraps of SL11 and an aluminium cigarette case made from the recovered wreckage of L70. The latter is engraved with the signature of Egbert Cadbury and was probably made as a gift for someone at the South Denes air station. Along with photographs and press cuttings, there is also a display about the South Denes base and a model showing how it looked.

See Caister-on-Sea.

King's Lynn

King's Lynn was raided a few hours after Great Yarmouth on the evening of 19 January 1915. It was attacked by *Kapitänleutnant* von Platen-Hallermund, commanding L4. He arrived over East Anglia mistaking it for the Humber area, his original target, and muddled his way along the north Norfolk coast. He aimed at a few villages – reported in a wireless message back to base as 'fortified places between the Tyne and the Humber' – and flew over Sandringham before stumbling upon King's Lynn. The town's Chief Constable, Charles Hunt, heard of a Zeppelin over the county and at 10.50 pm had the Electrical Engineer plunge the town into darkness, but it was too late. L4 had already seen its streetlights and followed the railway line into the town, its throbbing engines waking the inhabitants. Von Platen-Hallermund described the small town as an unidentified 'big city' and claimed to have begun bombing only after being shot at: a mistake or a lie as neither guns of any description nor planes defended King's Lynn at the time.

The Zeppelin dropped seven high explosives and one incendiary in its ten-minute raid. The third HE proved fatal, falling on a densely packed Victorian terrace in former Bentinck Street (now a car park between Blackfriars Street and St James's Street). It landed on numbers 11 and 12 destroying both houses and badly damaging others in the street. At number 12 was the Goate family: there, fourteen-year-old Percy was killed by shock. Next door, Mrs Alice Maud Gazley had been sheltering with the owners, Mr and Mrs Fayers, but had been so terrified by the sound of the German airship that she ran out into the street as the bomb exploded.

The ruined houses in Bentinck Street, King's Lynn, where Percy Goate and Alice Gazley died, 19 January 1915. Naval Zeppelin L4, under the command of Kapitänleutnant von Platen-Hallermund, was responsible. Imperial War Museum

The twenty-six-year-old widow, whose husband Percy had been killed in France only last October, received bruises to her face and leg, but she too was killed by shock rather than physical injury. Others in the two houses were dug out from beneath the rubble. The death certificates of the two killed duly attributed their deaths to 'the effects of the acts of the King's Enemies'.

Elsewhere in King's Lynn, bombs fell in Tennyson Avenue, East Street, Albert Street and Cresswell Street, as well as near the docks and close to the railway station. Thirteen were afterwards treated in hospital for their injuries, mainly cuts and lacerations. L4 crossed Norfolk on its way home and might have attacked Norwich if it had been visible, but blackout and mist hid the city.

In the days following the sortie on the town, unsubstantiated claims were made by a number of people to the effect that cars with dazzling lights had been seen at the time to signal and guide the attacking Zeppelin. Although police and intelligence enquiries yielded no evidence, the town's MP, Holcombe Ingleby, was certain spies had been afoot and published a pamphlet and letters to *The Times* stating his belief in the face of official denial.

Percy Goate and Alice Gazley were buried next to each other in King's Lynn Cemetery on consecutive

Mrs Alice Maud Gazley, killed during the air raid on King's Lynn, 19 January 1915. Only a couple of months before her death, her husband, Percy, had been killed on the Western Front. Imperial War Museum

The graves of Alice Gazley and Percy Goate, buried next to each other in King's Lynn Cemetery. Imperial War Museum

days, the former in a quiet ceremony, the latter attracting a large crowd. Their graves may be found in New Cemetery on the south side of Hardwick Road: follow the central path, cross the little bridge and they lie thirty yards to the right.

Objects associated with the First World War air raids are on display at the Town House Museum of Lynn Life, Queen Street. These include photographs of damage inflicted by L4, German airship wreckage made into swallow brooches and a ruler, and a notice from King's Lynn Electric Theatres advising cinema goers that a warning will appear on screen should Zeppelins or other enemy aircraft be reported in the district. Other notices, souvenirs and bomb fragments that are not on display may be viewed by appointment.

Sandringham

Oberleutnant zur See Frankenberg, commanding L21, was hoping to raid Norwich on 2/3 September 1916. He was unsure where he was over Norfolk, however, and released three bombs to test what, if any, defences were below him. The response provoked from the powerful searchlights and AA batteries at Sandringham took him aback. The remaining bomb load was discarded and the Zeppelin hastened away.

No damage resulted from the incident, but the Sandringham guns claimed to have hit the raider. Ignorant of Frankenberg's own mistake and the Germans' own ban on the bombing of royal palaces, the British presumed that the attack had been a deliberate attempt against Sandringham.

NORTHAMPTONSHIRE

Corby

On 1 October 1916 an AA battery near Corby fired on the passing L34, commanded by *Kapitänleutnant* Max Dietrich. Shells missed the Zeppelin, which was at 9,000ft, and enticed the raider into dropping seventeen high explosives in the assumption that the battery was defending something significant. The bombs fell in a line between Kirby Hall and the southern entrance of Corby railway tunnel. L34 then moved north-east and dropped thirteen incendiaries close to the Rockingham to Gretton road. No harm was done by any of these; instead, several were recovered and put on display to raise money for the Red Cross.

Northampton

There were twenty-nine air raid alarms and sixty-six bombs dropped in Northamptonshire in the First World War. Northampton was raided once, in the 'Silent Raid' of 19/20 October 1917. L45, commanded by *Kapitänleutnant* Kölle, was originally headed for Sheffield, but caught in a gale like the other naval Zeppelins that night, was driven south. The rudder-man, Heinrich Bahn, wrote afterwards:

> *I looked at my comrades in the car to see if I could read their thoughts, but only cold and anxiety were there... For nearly two hours we struggled to keep our westward course, but the wind blew ever stronger and I could tell that our navigation was getting more and more uncertain. We dropped a few bombs at some faint lights, but providence*

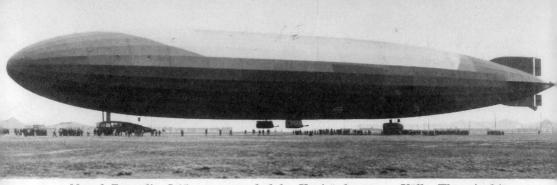

alone knows where they went. I scarcely believe that Leutnant Schutz, our second-in-command, troubled to set the bomb sight.

Kölle thought they had bombed Oxford, but those 'faint lights' were in fact Northampton. The Zeppelin had appeared over the northern suburbs at 10.45 pm, where five 50kg (110lb) bombs were dropped on Kingsthorpe and Dallington. A series of nine incendiaries followed, falling in Spencer Bridge Road, Victoria Park, Parkwood Road, Park Road, Corporation West Bridge Works and close to the railway line. Four explosives then landed at the Hunsbury Hill railway tunnel, a 100kg (220lb) and a 50kg device came down near Wootton Hill Farm and, lastly, three 50kg bombs struck the parishes of Preston Deanery and Piddington. Further away, Greens Norton and Towcester were also bombed.

Of the total of twenty-three bombs to fall on Northampton, only one proved fatal. This fell in the St James's End area at 46 Parkwood Street, where Mrs Eliza Gammons was killed immediately and her thirteen-year-old twin daughters were mortally injured. Gladys succumbed to burns and shock the next day, Lillian died two days later.

After raiding Northampton, Kölle went on to bomb London and inflicted many more casualties. However, he and his Zeppelin came to grief the following morning. Unable to return to Germany or escape to Switzerland, the airship made a forced landing at Sisteron in France and Kölle and his crew were taken prisoner. It is said that parts of the captured L45 eventually returned to Northamptonshire: apparently Brigadier General the Honourable Charles G Fortescue brought back fragments of the airship's aluminium to Pitsford, where he had the village blacksmith fashion them into souvenir ashtrays to be sold in aid of the troops.

See the entry for Piccadilly, Central London.

NORTH YORKSHIRE

Boulby

A sound mirror (circa 1916) exists on the western edge of the village of Boulby, on farmland beside the minor road that leads from the village to Upton and a hundred yards before reaching the radio mast at the top of the hill. Although there is no

The sound mirror at Boulby.

public access, the sound mirror is clearly visible from the road. The convex mirror is shielded by its projecting sides, designed to reduce interference.

For an explanation of sound mirrors see the entry for Kilnsea, East Riding of Yorkshire. For a similar sound mirror nearby see the entry for Redcar, below; for another further afield see Sunderland, Tyne & Wear.

Redcar

Like the sound locators at Boulby and Sunderland, this one is 'winged' to reduce interference. A Grade II* listed structure, its once uninterrupted view to the North Sea has been blocked by the surrounding Ings housing estate in a south-eastern suburb of the town, and it now stands on the corner of Greenstones Road and Holyhead Drive.

See the entry for Kilnsea, East Riding of Yorkshire, for an explanation of sound mirrors; see also Boulby, above, and Sunderland, Tyne & Wear.

The sound mirror at Redcar, not far away.

Skinningrove

Kapitänleutnant Loewe attempted to attack the benzol works at Skinningrove on 8 September 1915. He arrived here in L9 just after 9.30 pm and guessing, rather than certain, that he was over the plant, loosed several bombs. One explosive hit the benzol house (which contained 45,000 gallons) but it failed to penetrate the concrete roof; another blew up within feet of the same building, but did no more than scratch the structure. One bomb landed directly on the TNT store, but this proved a dud. If the storage tanks had been struck the entire place might have gone up. During the raid, workers from the plant sheltered in nearby mines.

L11 (*Korvettenkapitän* Schütze) made an opportunistic sortie against Skinningrove Iron Works on the night of 5/6 April 1916, after being deterred from Hull by AA, and prevented from reaching the secondary goal of Hartlepool by engine breakdowns. The most significant damage Schütze's twenty-nine explosives and incendiaries did was to demolish a laboratory at the works. No one was hurt on the ground and the Zeppelin flew away unmolested; lack of searchlights prevented the AA batteries from aiming one shot at it.

The iron works were targeted again a month later, on 2 May. The offender this time was *Kapitänleutnant* Otto von Schubert, commanding L23. The dozen bombs he dropped around 10.00 pm caused superficial damage to several buildings, but devices released on Easington, as L23 headed east out to sea, demolished a house and injured a child. Nearby, on the same night, Carlin How was bombed by *Kapitänleutnant* Ehrlich, commanding L17. A dozen high explosives and four incendiaries flattened six houses, but no one was badly hurt.

York

Kapitänleutnant der Reserve Max Dietrich, in L21, raided York on 2 May 1916. Although the assault lasted only ten minutes, this was the most serious raid on the city during the First World War and took place before AA or searchlights had been set up in its defence. Dietrich approached from Bishopthorpe at 10.30 pm and dropped a salvo of eighteen bombs on Dringhouses, shattering windows and wounding two soldiers. He then flew over York in a south-west to north-east diagonal. Bombs falling on Nunthorpe Hall Red Cross Hospital produced no casualties, but a subsequent device in Nunthorpe Avenue killed a girl, injured her sister in the spine and tore the arm off their mother. An explosive landing in Upper Price Street collapsed a house 'like a pack of cards', killing the elderly couple who lived there. Further

Kapitanleutnant der Reserve *Max Dietrich (left) who, in L21, carried out the first raid against York, on 2 May 1916; next to him is his watch officer,* Oberleutnant *Christian von Nathusius. Later in the year, on 27/28 November, Dietrich was shot down and killed off Hartlepool in another Zeppelin, L34, while L21 was destroyed off Lowestoft.*
Imperial War Museum

bombs fell in Caroline Street and damaged houses in Newton Terrace and Kyme Street, within the city walls. The Zeppelin next dropped an explosive on Peaseholme Green, killing five civilians and a soldier, and injuring one other person. Its remaining bombs fell in open fields outside the city. Dietrich went home in the belief that he had raided Middlesbrough.

Provisioning York with air defences prevented a repeat tragedy. Naval Zeppelin L14, commanded by *Hauptmann* Manger, approached from Fulford at 11.00 pm on 25 September, but was driven away from the centre by a gun and searchlight on a hill near Poppleton Road. Bombs were confined to the eastern outskirts of the city, where they damaged the church at Heworth. An old lady died of shock during the course of the raid, however.

On 27/28 November 1916 *Kapitänleutnant* Eichler, commanding L13, attacked York from the north after dropping bombs over Barmby Moor. His Zeppelin encountered intense anti-aircraft fire and was seen to have been hit as it wriggled in the searchlight beams. It climbed and retreated, leaving two explosives and twenty-one incendiaries behind it. These fell on the east of the city where some damage was caused to houses in Stanley Street, Fountayne Street and Wigginton Road, and two persons were slightly hurt. Incidentally, that night, Max Dietrich, who had been the first airship commander to assail York, was shot down in L34 off Hartlepool.

York Castle Museum, in the Eye of York, has air raid precaution notices, identification posters, Zeppelin fragments and a Ranken dart in its collection, but none of these are currently on display.

NOTTINGHAMSHIRE

Nottingham

The glow from Nottingham's blast furnace chimneys made the city an easy target for *Kapitänleutnant* Herman Kraushaar, commanding L17, when he raided between 12.00 and 1.00 am on 24 September 1916. Eight high explosives and eleven incendiaries were dropped on what Kraushaar thought was Sheffield, killing three and injuring seventeen. The Midland Railway freight station was wrecked and damage caused to the Great Central Railway Station and rail track. Bombs also afflicted Lister Gate, Greyfriar Gate and Broad Marsh. Little resistance was offered to the attack: a blanket of mist rising from the Trent obscured the German airship from below, while one of its bombs by fluke severed the telephone wires connecting the AA battery and searchlights at Sneinton, preventing their cooperation. That night, however, L17's crew had the unnerving experience of seeing their sister ship, L32, fall in flames a hundred miles away in Essex.

For the fate of L32 (*Oberleutnant zur See* Peterson) and L33 (*Kapitänleutnant der Reserve* Böcker), which also came down during the raid, see the entries for Great Burstead and Little Wigborough, both in Essex.

Retford

When a German airship was heard passing close to Retford on the evening of 2 September 1916 'alarm buzzers' were sounded, prompting many townspeople to leave the safety of their homes to see what was happening. Whether the noise of the warning drew the raider's attention to Retford, or whether it had already spotted railway lights there, *Kapitänleutnant* Prölss's L13 then dropped a flare to reveal the ground and attacked with fourteen bombs. Some fell in an orchard adjacent to three gasometers and peppered the containers with shrapnel, igniting all three. The blaze could be seen for miles and 'the heat from the flames baked the apples on the trees and roasted alive the roosting wild birds', according to the *Retford, Gainsborough and Worksop Times*. Witnesses claimed that a 'hearty cheer' could be heard from the Zeppelin crew at the sight of the conflagration.

Another explosive landed in front of the neighbouring house, which belonged to the gasworks' manager, blowing in its windows. Had anyone been in the rooms, which were riddled by glass and bomb fragments, they would surely have been killed or maimed; wisely, the family were in the cellar at the time. Not far away, other bombs damaged the roofs and windows of several cottages belonging to a man who had previously declined to insure them, on the grounds that there was not one chance in a million they would ever be damaged by a Zeppelin. The example of his misfortune triggered a rush on insurance services in the town the following Monday. Three women and three men were hurt in the raid, mostly as a result of flying debris. One of the women was hospitalized with serious head injuries; one of the men, who had dislocated a shoulder, ironically received his injury falling downstairs as he hurried to shelter.

SOUTH YORKSHIRE

Sheffield
The industrial city of Sheffield was one of the largest armaments producers in the Empire and was vital to the war effort. When a German Navy Zeppelin raided it on the night of 25/26 September 1916 bombs only narrowly missed the city's factories, striking closely built workers' houses instead. The raid was conducted by *Kapitänleutnant* Martin Dietrich in L22, who approached Sheffield from the southeast. The Zeppelin circled clockwise over the city before dropping incendiaries and high explosives in a south-easterly and then easterly direction over Pitsmoor and Attercliffe, suburbs north of the city centre.

The first bomb fell in Burngreave Cemetery, the second close to Danville Street where a man was killed. In Grimesthorpe Road, the next bomb split a house in two and killed its two elderly female inhabitants; at the corner of Petre Street and Lyons Road an old man was struck dead by shrapnel as he looked out of his window; an elderly woman died from wounds and shock caused by a bomb in Writtle Street. Nearing the heart of Sheffield's munitions works, two high explosives fell in rapid succession in Cossey Road. The first demolished three houses in a row and penetrated the cellar of the middle one, number 26, where four families were sheltering; three men, four women and three children were killed by the explosion. The second landed at number 10, blowing up a young couple and their baby son as they slept together in bed. In Corby Street, on the other side of the steel and iron works, a bomb accounted for a further nine victims, seven of them at number 136, where five of the family were children. A bomb in Princess Street demolished the Primitive Methodist Chapel, all except for one wall on which a text read above the

Shell production at Sir Robert Hadfield's Works in Sheffield. The city was essential to Britain's armaments industry. Imperial War Museum

ruins: 'A new commandment I give unto you, that ye love one another'. Further bombs fell close to the bridge beside Washford Road and in Woodbourn Road where a man in the street was blown up while warning a household to put out their lights. The Zeppelin finally disappeared east over Darnall, leaving behind twenty-eight dead and nineteen injured. The total could have been much worse. Sheffield's defences were afterwards described as a fiasco, no order having been given for AA to open fire during the raid. To address deficiencies, extra searchlights and guns were mounted on the hills around the city against future attacks.

Bitterness about the raid continued after the war. When a memorial was unveiled outside the Baltic Steel Works on Armistice Day 1922, it was intended to perpetuate the infamy of the Germans as much as remember the dead. The Chairman of the works told the large gathering assembled for the ceremony that if the Germans had had their way neither the works nor they would still exist. Although no longer a steelworks, the building and memorial still stand on Effingham Road, off Attercliffe Road. Fifty yards left of the Baltic Works entrance, the large grey stone set back in the brick wall reads:

> *'Lest we Forget' on September 26th 1916 nine men, ten women and ten children were killed by a German air raid on Sheffield. One of the bombs fell close to this spot.*

The bomb referred to is probably the one that landed near Washford Road.

STAFFORDSHIRE

Cannock Chase German War Cemetery

The German War Cemetery, or *Deutscher Soldatenfriedhof*, was built by the German War Graves Commission as a resting place for Germans who died on British territory in the two world wars. Publicly inaugurated on 10 June 1967, it is the only one of its kind in Great Britain. Of the 2,143 dead of the First World War, a number were killed carrying out air raids on the country. The crews of the airships that were brought down have their own special place of honour in the cemetery, in a raised and walled area on the right of where visitors enter. Here, buried in a row in the order of when they died, are those of SL11 commanded by *Hauptmann* Wilhelm Schramm, L32 commanded by *Oberleutnant zur See* Werner Peterson, L31 commanded by *Kapitänleutnant* Heinrich Mathy, and L48 commanded by *Kapitänleutnant der Reserve* Franz Eichler. Four simple stone slabs are engraved with their names and ranks.

Elsewhere in the cemetery lie the recovered crew members of L34 and L70, as well as Gotha airmen. The crew of the Gotha shot down at Wickford in Essex in 1918, *Leutnant* Friedrich von Thomsen and his two *Unteroffiziers*, Walter Heiden and Karl Ziegler, occupy a single grave in the otherwise Second World War half of the cemetery.

Cannock Chase lies between Stafford and Cannock. The German War Cemetery is near the middle of it.

Memorial to the fallen crewmen of German airships, buried at Cannock Chase German War Cemetery.

Christ Church Mission Room, Burton upon Trent, wrecked by a Zeppelin bomb on 31 January 1916. A missionary was delivering a lecture at the time of the explosion; she was killed along with five others. Imperial War Museum

Burton upon Trent

Burton was well lit on the evening of 31 January 1916 and paid the price for its complacency. Three separately attacking German Navy Zeppelins raided it within one hour. Historians have found it difficult to plot the raiders that night because their courses wavered and crossed each other in fog and cloud, while their commanders had no idea where they were. However, the first of the marauders to attack the town, at 8.45 pm, was probably *Kapitänleutnant* Stabbert, commanding L20. Having earlier bombed Loughborough, he dropped twelve incendiaries on Burton which left houses and two breweries badly damaged. His sortie was followed up by L15 under *Kapitänleutnant* Breithaupt, who dropped twenty-five bombs on what he mistakenly believed was Sheffield. *Kapitänleutnant* Loewe, in L19, carried out the third and final raid (later L19 came down in the North Sea with engine failure, all on board eventually drowning). An equal number of high explosives and incendiaries fell during the raid, but it is impossible to tell exactly which individual raiders dropped which ones. However, it is clear that most fell in and around the town centre, with the most destructive one exploding beside the Mission Room of Christ Church (now the Elim and Pentecostal Church) on the corner of Moore Street and Uxbridge Street. Mary Rose Morris, a guest missionary, was inside addressing a congregation of two hundred at the time. She was speaking, Bible in hand, of the Second Coming of Christ when the blast occurred, and died along with five of her audience. In all, fifteen people died immediately or as a result of their injuries, with a further seventy-two requiring treatment at Burton Infirmary.

Town officials had been warned that Zeppelins were near Derby and heading their

Bombed houses in Shobnall Street, Burton upon Trent. **Imperial War Museum**

way an hour before the first raid on Burton, but not all the streetlights were extinguished before the bombs began to fall. Even when conscientious locals shinned up lampposts or threw missiles to put them out, many shop lights and lamps in private houses, as well as the railway lights, remained on. As ever, fuller blackouts were imposed after the event and vain appeals were made to the War Office for better protection. Although several alarms bothered Burton's inhabitants in the following years, fortunately the Zeppelins never returned.

Other Midland towns and cities were raided the same evening as Burton upon Trent, the Naval Airship Division claiming that successful raids had been carried out against Liverpool – their primary goal that night. The reports of sunken ships, a wrecked powder factory and destroyed bridges and docks, however, was unfounded.

See the entries for Loughborough in Leicestershire, Ilkeston in Derbyshire, Birmingham and Walsall in the West Midlands, and Derby.

Stoke-on-Trent
Stoke-on-Trent was attacked on 31 January 1916 by naval Zeppelin L13, commanded by *Kapitänleutnant* Mathy. Seven high explosives were aimed at the glow of blast furnaces, but the only damage caused was to a few windows at Fenton Colliery. Returning eastward, Mathy attacked Scunthorpe.

See the entry for Scunthorpe, Lincolnshire.

166

SUFFOLK

Acton

An incendiary bomb dropped by an airship on the parish in 1916 is displayed in the tower of All Saints Church.

Bungay

During the night of 2/3 September 1916, when SL11 was brought down at Cuffley by William Leefe Robinson, *Kapitänleutnant* von Buttlar in L30 crossed the Suffolk coast at Lowestoft and dropped several bombs here. These opened up craters on Bungay Common where soldiers of the 62 West Riding Division of the Royal Engineers were encamped, but neither servicemen nor townspeople were hurt.

Not for the first time, von Buttlar inflated his deeds. On this occasion he claimed in his report that he had steered his Zeppelin up the Thames estuary and successfully attacked the City of London while under intense anti-aircraft fire and being pursued by aeroplanes. Von Buttlar in fact met no resistance and was nearly a hundred miles away from his pretended objective.

Naval Zeppelin L30, which raided Bungay on the night of 2/3 September 1916. The commander, Kapitänleutnant *von Buttlar, claimed he had attacked London.* Imperial War Museum

Bury St Edmunds

Bury St Edmunds was first bombed on 29/30 April 1915, Army Zeppelin LZ38 being the culprit. Commanded by *Hauptmann* Linnarz, the airship set off from Brussels-Evère and crossed the coast at Felixstowe. The Zeppelin dropped several incendiaries near Ipswich before flying inland as far as Bury, which it reached around midnight. It dropped its first high explosive on the north of the town, in Northgate Avenue, creating a huge crater close to the East Anglian School. From here Linnarz steered south and then zigzagged in a clockwise direction over the town centre, all the while dropping incendiaries. Premises were damaged in Northgate Street, Angel Hill and Lower Baxter Street. In Butter Market a device gutted Jeremiah Day's bootmakers at number 32, the fire spreading to neighbouring shops and raging out of control until morning. An auction room and stables at the corner of St Andrew's Street and King's Road were set alight, and further incendiaries fell on Crown Street, Southgate Street and fields south of Bury. Manoeuvring back over the town, the raider dropped bombs on Westgate Road, Hospital Road near the General Hospital (which many citizens convinced themselves was targeted on purpose) and the Boby Engineering Works. The Zeppelin set fire to a chicken coop in York Road, then departed to the west along Newmarket Road, dropping a second explosive and a series of incendiaries as it went. A third high explosive and more incendiaries were released as it swung south over the village of Westley; its last bombs fell on the hamlet of Woolpit as Linnarz turned east for the coast.

Bury had been defenceless on this still, clear night, but, considering the number of bombs, it is surprising that there were no casualties other than a dog consumed in the fire in Butter Market. Had Linnarz used more explosives instead of firebombs the toll would have been higher. As it was, this was the first German Army airship raid on the country; a month later Linnarz and LZ38 were to become the first to bomb London.

Bury endured a second, and much worse, air raid nearly a year later on 31 March/1 April 1916. This time the airship was a naval Zeppelin, *Oberleutnant zur See* Peterson's L16. Eight explosives and a pair of incendiaries were dropped on the town in the space of fifteen minutes, most falling west of the town centre in a north-south course along Spring Lane, Chalk Lane (now Chalk Road North) and Mill Road. Private Hubert Hardiment, who was on leave, was killed at the back door of his landlady's house as he went to investigate the attack; Harry Frost was fatally wounded as he watched the raid in his garden; at another house a blast killed Mrs Dureall, whose husband was away serving with the 3 Suffolk Regiment, and two of her five children, aged three and five, in her bedroom. Elsewhere in Bury bombs landed near the railway line by Eastgate Street, behind St Mary's Vicarage at the top of Southgate Street and beside Prussia Lane. In the last place the elderly Henry Adams and his fifteen-year-old son died. It was a bad night for Suffolk: the same evening *Kapitänleutnant der Reserve* Böcker in L14 bombed Sudbury and *Kapitänleutnant* Mathy in L13 raided Stowmarket, claiming more victims in the county. (See the entries for Stowmarket and Sudbury.)

Moyse's Hall Museum on Cornhill has in its collection a recovered incendiary, postcards relating to the raids, and commemorative china models of Zeppelin bombs, made as souvenirs at the time and decorated with coats of arms. Although not usually on display, an appointment can be made to view them.

Felixstowe

Felixstowe and neighbouring Harwich were attacked several times during the war. The two most notable raids occurred in July 1917. At around 7.30 am on the morning of the 4th eighteen Gothas attacked Felixstowe and Harwich, killing nine and wounding nineteen at the RNAS base, and destroying a Curtiss H12 'Large America' Flying Boat. The England Squadron carried out another early morning raid on the 22nd, twenty-one Gothas claiming thirteen lives and injuring twenty-six, most casualties being soldiers of the Suffolk Regiment at a nearby army base.

Earlier in the war, on the night of 13/14 September 1915, AA from the town nearly brought down Zeppelin L13, commanded by Mathy, when a lucky shot into clouds by a 6-pounder struck the airship's gangway. Two gas cells were damaged and the radio power cable and fuel line were cut, forcing Mathy to discard his bomb load and limp home via Holland. On the morning of 14 June 1917 a H12 Flying Boat flew from RNAS Felixstowe and engaged L43 which was scouting over the North Sea, near the Dutch island of Vlieland. The flying boat stole up on the Zeppelin's tail at 2,000ft and, after two bursts of Brock and Pomeroy bullets above the tail, the airship caught fire and plummeted into the sea, some of the crew leaping from the burning wreckage on its way down. The 'boat' was flown by Flight Sub-Lieutenant

Flight Sub-Lieutenant Culley making the first successful take-off from a lighter towed behind a destroyer. The trial, which took place out of Felixstowe, on 31 July 1918, proved significant. Repeating the process two weeks later, further out to sea, Culley shot down Zeppelin L53 off the Dutch coast. Imperial War Museum

B. D. Hobbs, with Flight Sub-Lieutenant R. F. L. Dickey manning the bow gun that downed the airship; the other two crew were Air Mechanics H M Davies and A W Goody.

To the south of Felixstowe stands Landguard Fort, overlooking the Orwell Estuary and guarding the approach to Felixstowe and Harwich harbours. A number of anti-aircraft guns were based around the fort in the First World War, and the RNAS base was situated a couple of hundred yards away, towards Felixstowe docks. Today, Felixstowe Museum occupies Ravelin Block adjoining the fort. Among its exhibits is a 6lb shell fired by naval forces during the raid on 22 July 1917 – the shell missed the German aeroplanes and fell in Old Felixstowe church, landing on the organ – a Public Warning aircraft recognition poster, and a case and fuses of 1lb 'pom pom' shells, of the type that were ineffectually employed as AA at the start of the war.

Lowestoft

The port was raided on the evening of 15 April 1915 by *Kapitänleutnant der Reserve* Böcker in Navy airship L5. He flew low over the town, at less than 5,000ft, but there was nothing to repel him – rifle and revolver fire was harmless. Incendiaries and explosives fell around the harbour and set light to a timber yard.

Lowestoft Maritime Museum on Whapload Road possesses two small propeller fragments taken from fallen Zeppelins. One belongs to L21, which was shot down off the coast by Flight Lieutenant Cadbury and Flight Sub-Lieutenant Pulling in the early morning of 28 November 1916; the other piece is part of L33 which came down at Little Wigborough in Essex in September 1916.

Shells from the naval bombardment of the town in April 1916 are also on display, along with information relating to the anti-U-boat campaign in which the fishing smacks and sailors of this harbour town were much involved.

Newmarket

Oberleutnant zur See Peterson, in L16, arrived over East Anglia at 10.15 pm on the evening of 24 April 1916. He flew by Kimberley, where he dropped a bundle of German illustrated newspapers, then over Thetford, arriving at Newmarket at around 12.30 am on 25 April. Coming under machine-gun fire, he directed twenty bombs against the market town, which he thought was Cambridge. Eighteen explosives fell across the centre of Newmarket, razing five houses and damaging a hundred more. Only one person was injured, however, and the only fatality that night was Coup de Main, a champion racehorse, killed in its stables on Bury Road. Peterson dropped another high explosive and an incendiary outside the town, then departed at speed to the north-east.

Somersham

St Mary's Church has an incendiary bomb that was dropped in nearby Nettlestead by a German airship. It is hung on a wall of the nave.

Stowmarket

Stowmarket was raided on the evening of 31 March 1916 by *Kapitänleutnant* Mathy, in command of L13. He was heading for London and wanted somewhere to shed bombs in order to lighten his airship and attain an altitude of relative safety. He chose Stowmarket after following the lights of a train from Ipswich to the town, and because the New Explosive Works was there. When he arrived he dropped parachute flares to locate the works, but only succeeded in arousing anti-aircraft fire. Mathy released bombs to silence the battery, unaware that he was directly above the explosives factory. The twelve high explosives that landed there, however, merely shattered a few windows. The Zeppelin circled while a second attempt was made to find the works, and came under fire again. This time the guns perforated gas cells amidships and in the nose of the airship. All hope of raiding London was abandoned and the crew's energy was concentrated on repairing the leaks and getting back to base at Hage. The good conduct of the German airmen was later highly praised in the commander's report.

The British learned next morning that Mathy's Zeppelin had been hit when a copy of a message written by Mathy, to be radioed back to Naval Staff, was found. The note had presumably been blown overboard.

Elsewhere in Suffolk, on the night of 31 March/1 April 1916, L16 (*Oberleutnant zur See* Peterson) raided Bury St Edmunds and L14 (*Kapitänleutnant der Reserve* Böcker) attacked Sudbury. (See the entries for Bury St Edmunds and Sudbury.)

Sudbury

Kapitänleutnant der Reserve Böcker, accompanied on board by Strasser, raided Sudbury on 31 March 1916 in L14. The attack began at 10.30 pm, the Zeppelin dropping eight high explosives and nineteen incendiaries as it flew east to west above the town, which was thought to be Cambridge. After the first bomb fell near the town cemetery, subsequent devices struck East Street, Constitution Hill, Newman's Road, Melford Road and Brunden meadows. In East Street, where a couple of houses were flattened, a man and two women were killed, while another man died in the street. On Constitution Hill a soldier was blown up and another gravely injured. Afterwards, L14 moved south-west to Braintree where it dropped another three explosives just after 11.00 pm, killing four and wounding seven.

A memorial outside St Gregory's Church on Gregory Street bears the names of those killed in Sudbury: John Edward Smith, Ellen Ambrose, Thomas Ambrose, Ellen Wheeler and Valentine Wilson. (The memorial was originally on North Street.)

For other Suffolk towns bombed the same night see the entries for Bury St Edmunds and Stowmarket.

Theberton

Holly Tree Farm, along Church Road, is where the last German airship was shot down on British soil. L48, under *Kapitänleutnant der Reserve* Eichler, was involved in a raid on 16/17 June 1917, its bombs falling without harm north of Harwich. Compelled by engine trouble to fly lower than was safe, it was caught by several British aeroplanes and brought down in flames at 3.30 am. The RFC airmen who between them shared the success were Lieutenant F. D. Holder and gunner Sergeant S. Ashby in a FE2b, Captain Robert Saundby in a DH2, and Lieutenant Pierce Watkins in a BE12. Watkins alone received the credit, however.

One of the two German crewmen to survive the blaze and make a full recovery was *Leutnant zur See* Otto Mieth. He was busy deciphering a weather report from

The crumpled remains of Zeppelin L48 near Theberton in Suffolk. The commander, Kapitänleutnant der Reserve *Franz Eichler, died in the crash but three of his men survived. Notice the sentries posted along inner and outer cordons to keep out souvenir hunters.* Imperial War Museum

Bruges when the Zeppelin was attacked – just as he stepped out of the wireless compartment and into the control car 'the whole ship was lit up as light as day'. Instinctively he stepped back and closed the door. He lost consciousness in the crash and would have burned to death except that the wireless cabin caught in a tall tree and avoided the rest of the burning wreckage. His thighs were broken in the fall, but at least he was alive: the wireless operator alongside him in the compartment was dead, with a broken spine. Although machinist Wilhelm Uecker survived the crash, he died as a result of his injuries over a year later on Armistice Day 1918.

A substantial portion of the framework of L48 is displayed in a glass case in the porch of St Peter's Church in Theberton. Photographs and an account of the Zeppelin's demise are below it. Before their removal to Cannock Chase German War Cemetery, the crew were buried in a single grave in the churchyard extension opposite Jubilee Hall. Their gravestone is no longer there, but a modern plaque on the left-hand side bears the quotation from Romans 14:4 which was charitably applied by a RFC chaplain at the time: 'Who art thou that judgest another man's servant?'

172

In the nearby town of Leiston, more reminders of L48 may be found at the Long Shop Steam Museum on Main Street. Accompanying a display about the airship's last flight is recovered aluminium, with some smaller pieces fashioned into ashtrays and brooches, including a Zeppelin-shaped one. An officer's glove, a button and safety matches collected from the crew are also on view, as well as incendiary bombs dropped in the county by other airships during the war. Garretts of Leiston, the engineering firm whose factory and machinery are the basis of the Museum, were sub-contracted in 1917 to build FE2b aircraft and there is also a display regarding this.

Woodbridge

Woodbridge was bombed by the German Navy's L10, commanded by *Oberleutnant zur See* Friedrich Wenke, on 12 August 1915. Having crossed the coast at Orfordness, the Zeppelin dropped twenty-four high explosives and incendiaries on the town at 10.30 pm, killing seven and injuring twenty-three. St John's Hill sustained the worst of the damage with a number of houses being demolished. L10's remaining bombs were destined for Harwich where a further seventeen people were hurt.

Woodbridge Museum on Market Hill has a display about the raid that includes photographs of the material destruction, a bomb fragment, a schoolgirl's eyewitness account and a cap lost by one of the Zeppelin's crew as they flew over the town. The display also has structural fragments and a 'Pictorial Souvenir of the "strafed" Zeppelin L48', the airship which was brought down at Theberton, some fifteen miles away. (See the preceding entry for Theberton.)

TYNE & WEAR

Newcastle upon Tyne

When *Kapitänleutnant* Hirsch suddenly arrived on Tyneside at half past midnight on 16 June 1915 he was unexpected and unresisted. The works and factories along the river were brightly lit up, inviting attack; there were no searchlights and the only fire directed against the raider came from an old cruiser guarding the Tyne, HMS *Brilliant*, which was ineffectual. As a result, Hirsch's L10 took its time to direct its bombs, first targeting Wallsend, where the Eastern Marine Engineering Works were considerably damaged. The Zeppelin then crossed to the south side of the river and ravaged Palmer's shipyard at Jarrow, high explosives claiming the lives of seventeen workers and wounding another seventy-two. Returning to the north bank, bombs struck Pochin's Chemical Works, then houses at Willington, where a policeman was blown up. Satisfied with his half-hour's work, Hirsch departed southwards, the airship dropping its remaining bombs on collieries at South Shields. When he passed out to sea, Hirsch reported that 'The glare from the raided locality was still visible 30 nautical miles away'.

This was the first air raid carried out using radio bearings, but the direction-finding stations built at Nordholz and Borkum were too much in a line with L10 to be of practical use. Further, more dispersed, stations were planned around Germany's North Sea coast and occupied Belgium to improve accuracy. Newcastle received two 12-pounder mobile guns as a result of the raid and the Royal Navy

Eastern Marine Engineering Works, Wallsend, bombed on 16 June 1915 by Kapitänleutnant *Hirsch, in Zeppelin L10.* Imperial War Museum

transferred twelve 6-inch guns from ships to shore, mounting them on railway trucks to be stationed in sidings along the coast.

Earlier in 1915, on 14 April, Wallsend had been visited by *Kapitänleutnant* Mathy in L9. Two people were slightly injured and an incendiary bomb damaged a house. Later, on 8/9 August 1916, L11 (*Korvettenkapitän* Schütze) raided Whitley Bay with thirteen bombs, injuring a woman and three children and causing minor damage to property. The Zeppelin was pursued at a distance by Flight Lieutenant Bruno de Roeper, in a BE2c from RNAS Redcar, but he lost it in fog twenty miles out to sea.

Sunderland

Sunderland was attacked around 11.00 pm on the evening of 1 April 1916, by L11 under *Korvettenkapitän* Schütze. The Zeppelin approached from the west, along the Wear, and scattered explosives and incendiaries on the Hylton Road, Millfield and Deptford areas before switching its attention to Monkwearmouth on the north side of the river. A railway goods yard at Wreath Quay was hit and a train carriage wrecked, the Thomas Street schools were damaged and a tram and a house were blown up in North Bridge Street. Other bombs fell in Victor Street, struck the Workmen's Hall in Whitburn Street and damaged St Benet's Church. A single shot fired by a gun at Fulwell in defence of Sunderland missed and the harbour was hit as the bomber headed out to sea. Schütze then flew south to drop further bombs in the vicinity of Middlesbrough.

During the few minutes that L11 took to cross the city it claimed twenty-two lives,

Naval Zeppelin L11, patrolling the North Sea. On 1 April 1916, commanded by Korvettenkapitän *Schütze, this airship carried out a raid on Sunderland.*
Imperial War Museum

Sunderland's sound mirror.

among them a magistrate who was the leader of the local Labour party. Another twenty-five were gravely hurt, some of whom died in the next few days, and over a hundred more were less seriously injured. Ghastly, disfigured bodies in the streets caused distress both to survivors and those tending them. Meanwhile, unscrupulous young men in the Causeway looted the shops that had been blown in.

Still standing in Sunderland, there is a concrete sound mirror similar to those found at Boulby and Redcar, though more weathered and overgrown. It is found beside a public footpath running north of the Fulwell windmill, on Carley Hill. The listening post once stood in an isolated position with a splendid prospect of the North Sea,'something which urban expansion now obscures. A plaque affixed to one side details the mirror's purpose.

For an explanation of sound mirrors see the entry for Kilnsea, East Riding of Yorkshire; see also Boulby and Redcar, both in North Yorkshire.

WEST MIDLANDS

Birmingham

This centre of munitions production experienced three raids in the First World War, but thankfully all of them were light, and although these produced spy scares, commendably in Birmingham there were no serious attacks on naturalized Germans or German businesses in their aftermath. The city had been quick to impose lighting restrictions and in January 1915 had organized a public warning sounded by factory steam whistles and hooters. These precautions were only tested a year later when, on 31 January/1 February 1916, several Zeppelins skirted the suburbs. Birmingham's blackout showed its worth as the city proper remained unmolested while the neighbouring Black Country towns that were less darkened were bombed. *Kapitänleutnant der Reserve* Max Dietrich, in L21, reported dropping thirty-five 50kg (110lb) explosives and twenty incendiaries with good results on what he thought was Liverpool and Birkenhead: having been blown south-east seventy miles off target by a tail wind, he actually struck Tipton, Wednesbury and Walsall, causing thirty-three dead and twenty injured. Soon afterwards, his colleague in L19, *Kapitänleutnant* Loewe – who, like Dietrich, misjudged himself to be over Liverpool – bombed the same districts, but without adding to the number of casualties. It was while returning from this raid that L19 came down in the North Sea.

Although Birmingham escaped harm that night, there was displeasure with the government that no official air raid warning had been received. Such indignation was felt throughout the Midlands that Birmingham's Lord Mayor, Neville Chamberlain, called a meeting of Mayors and Chief Constables in the region and made a personal representation to the Home Secretary. As a result, other towns adopted the same light restrictions as Birmingham and more anti-aircraft guns and better searchlights were installed on the city's surrounding hills. Still, by that summer, when the Home Office held a conference in Birmingham on the issue, an adequate early warning system had yet to be arranged.

During the 'Silent Raid' of 19/20 October 1917 the city centre was spared again by its obscurity when L41 under *Hauptmann* Manger passed over at 11.00 pm. Bombs fell on open country and the western suburbs, one hitting the Austin Works

Damage in Union Street, Tipton, after a raid on 31 January/1 February 1916.
The bomber was Kapitänleutnant der Reserve *Max Dietrich, in L21. He also*
attacked Wednesbury and Walsall in the area. Imperial War Museum

at Longbridge where two people were injured. The raid justified continued lighting restrictions which some had wanted to be relaxed.

Hauptmann Manger returned to Birmingham for another try late in the evening of 12 April 1918, this time commanding L62. He reported dropping 2½ tons of bombs on the city, which he thought had torn huge craters in the streets. His bombs actually caused little effect, most of them being dumped over Hockley Heath outside the city boundary. His Zeppelin was deterred from approaching closer to the centre by synchronized fire from the city's AA – the gunners' accuracy had been honed during rehearsals in Birmingham's very own air raid 'theatre' that cost £200 and took four months to erect. Ascending out of their range, L62 retreated towards Lapworth where its remaining bombs fell on a golf course and in fields. Lieutenant C H Noble-Campbell of No. 38 Squadron then pursued it in a FE2b for half an hour until he was wounded in the head and forced down at Coventry. For a long time it was supposed that the airship's guns were responsible – which would have made it the single occasion on which an attacking plane was beaten in combat with a Zeppelin – but as Manger and his crew made no mention of fending off an aeroplane, it is more likely that the British pilot was hurt by a bursting AA shell.

For other locations raided on the night of 31 January/1 February 1916 see the entries for Derby, Burton upon Trent in Staffordshire, Loughborough in Leicestershire and the following one for Walsall.

Walsall

There was no warning or blackout and the trams were running when Walsall was raided by *Kapitänleutnant der Reserve* Max Dietrich on the evening of 31 January 1916. The first bomb to fall from his Zeppelin, L21, struck the Congregational Church on Wednesbury Road at 8.00 pm. Children in the parlour at the time escaped without injury, other than to their nerves, but there was much damage to the roof, pews, floor and windows of the church, and outside in the street a Mr Thomas Merrylees was killed. An incendiary followed outside the General Hospital, but this was quickly put out. The third and fourth devices released by L21 damaged properties in Mountrath Street. In Bradford Place another bomb excavated a huge crater and injured a number of people. Among those sprayed with shrapnel were passengers on a tram, including Mrs Mary Slater, the town's Mayoress. Her chest and abdominal wounds ultimately proved fatal and she died three weeks later on 20 February. At least two others hurt in the incident also died.

The damage to surrounding buildings on Bradford Place was severe and a piece of shrapnel is still evident today, embedded and framed in the wall of the former Labour Club (known as Newton House at the time of the raid). On the main staircase of the Council House (Town Hall) a plaque commemorates Mrs Slater. Ironically, the Mayoress was part-German on her mother's side. Her grandfather was from Bremen.

See the entries for Derby, Burton upon Trent in Staffordshire, Loughborough in Leicestershire and Birmingham, above.

Highworth

St Michael's Church, next to the High Street, contains the family chapel of the Warnefords. On the south side of the chancel, it is filled with memorials, heraldic devices and tombstones from the seventeenth century onwards. A monument dedicated specifically to Reginald Warneford VC, the British pilot first to shoot down a German airship (Army Zeppelin LZ37), is on the north wall of the chapel, near the altar. The sculpture features a Victoria Cross, *Legion d'Honneur* (awarded by the French nation), RNAS wings and the family coat of arms.

See Brompton Cemetery in Central London: Warneford was buried there following a fatal flying accident on 17 June 1915, just ten days after his valiant action.

The memorial in St Michael's Church, Highworth, to Flight Sub-Lieutenant Warneford VC.

SCOTLAND

ABERDEENSHIRE

Craig Castle

During a planned assault against the naval base at Rosyth and the Forth Bridge on 2/3 May 1916, only two out of eight Naval Airship Division Zeppelins managed to reach Scotland, wind forcing the others to attack secondary objectives in the Midlands. Of the two, one was L20, commanded by *Kapitänleutnant* Stabbert; the other was L14 under *Kapitänleutnant der Reserve* Böcker. While Böcker confined himself to the Tay Estuary, Stabbert penetrated far inland where he became lost in snow and fog, an iced-up antenna foiling radio bearings. At midnight L20 was over Loch Ness and from here Stabbert headed south and then east over the Highlands.

Naval Zeppelin L20, wrecked on the Norwegian coast as it returned from a raid on Scotland on 2/3 May 1916. **Kapitänleutnant** *Stabbert was interned along with most of his crew, but he later escaped back to Germany.* Imperial War Museum

Lights at Craig Castle, near Lumsden, and far north of the restricted lighting area, were spotted by the crew and taken to be those of a mine head. Seventeen bombs were dropped on the target, but there were no direct hits. Minimal damage was caused and no one was hurt.

After leaving the coast at Peterhead, one hundred miles north of where Stabbert thought he was, the Zeppelin was faced with mounting head winds. With insufficient fuel to return to Germany, or even reach the sea off Denmark where German cruisers could have sailed to meet him, the commander had no choice but to set a course for neutral Norway. L20 reached the Norwegian coast south of Stavanger next morning, where, owing to the hazards posed by the mountainous terrain, an attempt was made to land in a fjord. Some of the crew scrambled out as soon as the Zeppelin pitched into the water, others quickly following as the airship drifted towards jagged cliffs. Six crew members who were plucked from the sea by local fishermen were repatriated as shipwrecked mariners, but those who swam ashore were interned. Stabbert was among the latter, but he escaped later that year and made it back to Germany.

Craig Castle is in private hands and is not open to the public. See the entry for Edinburgh, below, for more about *Kapitänleutnant der Reserve* Böcker in Scotland.

EDINBURGH

Edinburgh
The Scottish capital was attacked by two naval Zeppelins on 2/3 April 1916. The first to reach Edinburgh that night was L14, commanded by *Kapitänleutnant der Reserve* Böcker. He had first-hand knowledge of the district, having visited the port before the war as an officer of the Hamburg-Amerika shipping line, but from the air he was unable to locate Forsyth dockyard or the Forth Bridge, which were his original targets. Fired on by destroyers in the Firth of Forth he moved inland to Leith at 11.30 pm where his bombs killed a man and a child. Among the properties that were damaged around the port was Messrs. Innes and Grieve's whisky warehouse, which burned to the ground with its bottled contents valued at £44,000. Like a good many other buildings damaged that night, it was uninsured against raids, Scotsmen and women thinking themselves safe so far north.

Although a warning had been issued as early as 9.00 pm in Edinburgh, bringing all road and rail traffic to a halt, and the fact that the explosions in Leith could be clearly heard, many of its citizens refused to believe that the Germans had really arrived and were attacking until they saw the Zeppelin for themselves. Böcker duly quashed their doubts by flying over the Old Town at ten to twelve for part two of his raid. Shops were wrecked and house windows smashed along Lauriston Place and a man killed there by shrapnel. In Archibald Place a high explosive fell in the playground of George Watson's College, smashing classrooms on the ground and first floors. Circling east and north, L14 then dropped an incendiary which landed beside the boiler room of the Edinburgh Royal Infirmary. On the north side of Grassmarket five floors of the White Hart Hotel were wrecked and a person there killed and four injured; the Corn Exchange on the south side was also badly damaged. A bomb near Edinburgh Castle burst on rock facing Castle Terrace,

Crowds viewing the air raid damage in Grassmarket, Edinburgh. On the left of the picture is the White Hart Hotel where one person was killed and four injured. Kapitänleutnant der Reserve Bocker, in L14, carried out the raid on the Scottish capital on 2/3 April 1916. Imperial War Museum

Damage to the roof of McCallum's Bonded Store in Haddon Court, Edinburgh. Imperial War Museum

blowing out windows and uprooting trees. The County Hotel and other properties in Lothian Road were blasted by further bombs. Böcker then crossed over the city from west to east. Resuming the onslaught, an explosive killed five people at the foot of a tenement stairs in Marshall Street, and a girl was blown up in St Leonard's Hill. Elsewhere in the city, bomb damage was recorded in Haddon Court behind Nicholson Street, Kings Road and Kings Park, Bedford Place, Coltbridge Gardens, East Claremont Street and at Princes Street railway station.

Because there were no anti-aircraft guns in Edinburgh Böcker had been able to descend as low as 2,200ft during the raid; the only resistance his Zeppelin encountered was from soldiers at the Castle with ineffective rifle fire. When he departed at 12.15 am a second raider arrived in the form of L22 (*Kapitänleutnant* Martin Dietrich) at high altitude. This Zeppelin caused no further harm, however, despite the three high explosives which Dietrich released on the south of the city. Earlier in the evening L22 had dropped explosives near Lamberton, Berwick-upon-Tweed, and incendiaries on agricultural land near Chirnside. None of them was any more successful than those dropped on Edinburgh, but Dietrich went home claiming to have ravaged Newcastle. The following day AA batteries arrived in Edinburgh, too late for the thirteen awaiting burial and the twenty-four recovering from their injuries.

Böcker returned to Scotland on 2/3 May, again commanding L14, for another attempt at the Forth Bridge. Half an hour before midnight he mistook the lights of fishing boats in the Tay Estuary for those of warships at anchor in the Firth of Forth. He aimed five high explosives at these, but missed them altogether, his bombs falling on fields outside Arbroath. Unable to find another target, he retired to Germany with the rest of his bombs still on board.

The National War Museum at Edinburgh Castle has in its collections fragments of the bombs dropped on Edinburgh and Leith, but these are not on display.

Bibliography

Heinrich Bahn, 'In a German Airship over England', *Journal of the Royal United Services Institute*, Vol. LXXI, London, 1926

Horst Freiherr Treusch von Buttlar, *Zeppelins Over England* (London, G. G. Harrap & Co.,1931)

H. G. Castle, *Fire Over England, The German Raids of World War I* (London, Leo Cooper in association with Secker & Warburg, 1982)

Christopher Cole and E. F. Cheesman, *The Air Defence of Britain 1914-1918* (London, Bodley Head, 1984)

Major Raymond H. Fredette, *The First Battle of Britain 1917-1918* (London, Cassell, 1966)

Mary Gibson, *Warneford VC* (Yeovil, Friends of the Fleet Air Arm Museum, 1979)

G. W. Haddow & Peter M. Grosz, *The German Giants, The German R-Planes 1914-1918* (London, Putnam, 3rd edition 1988)

Gareth Jenkins, *Zeppelins over Bury* (Bury St Edmunds, Moyse's Hall Museum, 1985)

Neville Jones, *The Origins of Strategic Bombing, A Study of the Development of British Air Strategic Thought and Practice up to 1918* (London, William Kimber, 1973)

Michael MacDonagh, *In London During the Great War* (London, Eyre and Spottiswoode, 1935)

Rolf Marben (ed.), *Zeppelin Adventures* (translated by Claud W. Sykes, London, John Hamilton, 1931)

Frank Morison, *War on Great Cities* (London, Faber & Faber, 1937)

Captain Joseph Morris, *The German Air Raids on Great Britain, 1914-1918* (London, Sampson Low, Marston & Co., 1925)

Georg Paul Neumann, *The German Air Force in the Great War* (London, Hodder & Stoughton, 1920; translated from the German by J. E. Gurdon)

Kenneth Poolman, *Zeppelins over England* (London, Evans Brothers, 1960)

Sir Walter Raleigh and H.A. Jones, *The War in the Air* (Oxford, Clarendon Press, 1922-1937)

Sir Alfred Rawlinson, *The Defence of London 1915-1918* (London, Andrew Melrose, 1923)

Raymond Laurence Rimell, *Zeppelin! A Battle for Air Supremacy in World War I* (London, Conway Maritime Press, 1984)

Douglas H. Robinson, *The Zeppelin in Combat* (Henley-on-Thames, G. T. Foulis & Co., 3rd edition, 1971)

David J. Smith, *Britain's Aviation Memorials & Mementoes* (Yeovil, Patrick Stephens Ltd., 1992)

Peter J. Smith, *Zeppelins over Lancashire, The story of the air raids on the county of Lancashire in 1916 and 1918* (Radcliffe, Manchester, Neil Richardson, 1991)

Nigel Steel & Peter Hart, *Tumult in the Clouds, The British Experience of The War in the Air, 1914-1918* (London, Hodder and Stoughton, 1997)

H.G. Wells, *The War in the Air* (London, T. Nelson & Sons, 1914, originally published 1908)

C. M. White, *The Gotha Summer, The German daytime air raids on England, May to August 1917* (London, Robert Hale, 1986)

Index